Costessey
A look into the past

Ernest G. Gage

By the same author – *Costessey Hall,* published 1991

Costessey - A look into the past
First Published 2002

Publisher - Brian Gage
31 Eastern Avenue
Norwich NR7 0UQ

ISBN 0-9542113-0-8

Typeset & printed by Catton Print of Norwich

ABOUT THE AUTHOR

After the publication of his first book in 1991, on the history of *Costessey Hall*, Ernest put his thoughts to the writing of a book dealing with all the old properties of the village, many of which are still standing. Going through the Tithe Plans of 1840 and ordnance maps of 1880 onwards he produced a plan to enable him to visit all the properties that where still standing in order to get the up-to-date information. This was an enormous task to undertake which he eventually completed in 1997. As a result an interesting history of all these old properties and their occupants have been beautifully described in this his second book *Costessey – A look into the past*.

The publisher wishes to thank the Eastern Evening News for their permission to use the above photograph of the author taken by HARRY NAYLOR.

Contents

Index

Index continued overleaf

Index

PREFACE

In October 1982 I compiled, on behalf of the Costessey Society, a list of all buildings considered to be of historic interest in the village of Costessey. This was to comply with the Secretary of State for the Environment's guidelines. These lists have been used for this record but have been extended to include all properties listed in the 1840 Tithe Award, and the text has been arranged in order that the reader can be taken on a phototgraphic tour of the village as it would have been between the mid 1800 period and the early 1900 period. Where old photographs have not been available, present day photographs have been used, and as these were taken in 1995 they have not been dated after their identification number which coincides with the section number under which a full description can be found.

Most of the buildings had been recorded in the 'Gunton Papers' produced by H.E. Gunton after he had retired from the post of Parish Clerk in 1958. He had used photographs produced by two earlier photographers, Francis Welch, postmaster of Costessey 1906-1942, and Ernest Ottaway, baker and grocer, Central Stores, Costessey 1901-1920. All of this work had been lodged at the Norwich Central Library and destroyed in the multi-million pound blaze in August 1994. Fortunately, in 1990, I spent many days in the Norwich Central Library photographing on to negative film all the photographs pertaining to the 'Gunton Papers' and these negatives can now be used to replace all those lost in the blaze. In addition, photographs offered to me when interviewing the occupiers of the old houses, together with those taken by Hallam Ashley FRPS, a Costessey photographer in 1951 and myself in 1995, are included in this record.

In 1970 the Costessey Society presented a copy of the 'Gunton Papers' to the Costessey Branch Library. Tim East, Parish Councillor, obtained a copy of this and loaned it to me, and Group Capt. Ron Hill presented me with his copy of the 1839 Tithe Award map. These records have been. researched, all properties identified and the Tithe Award number shown against the heading of each section as is the letter (L), where applicable, which indicates that the property is a listed building. Also, in 1994, the office of Messrs Pomeroy and Sons, the Costessey Estate solicitors, of Wymondham was cleared of all Estate documents which were passed over to me as temporary custodian. They contained much historical information which has been included in this record.

vii

Thanks are due to the many Costessey residents who were very helpful during my interviews with them, especially those who loaned me their photographs of the past. My grateful thanks are also due to Mrs Sylvia Yates who has read through this record and, with regard to its literary composition, has suggested improvements, and to Mr Tim East who has explored various avenues regarding the publication of this book on "Costessey – A look into the past".

Ernest G. Gage
Costessey

December 1997

Short History Of Costessey

Costessey is pleasantly situated in the valley of the River Wensum. It is difficult to trace the name of Costessey as Domesday records it as Costesela whilst the British Museum has records quoting the name as Costesseia. Other names listed in the Norwich Records Office are Costessie Compata and also Cofsey, Cossie and Cossese. Oliver Cromwell quoted the name as Cossey in his directives to his army in January 1648.

The old Manor House, now known as Costessey Park House, was built about 1450 and is the oldest building in Costessey. The first "New Hall" was built by Sir Henry Jernegan in 1565 and enlarged by Sir George Jerningham (note change of name) after he had obtained the Barony of Stafford in 1825. He was then known as Lord Stafford. Because of no male heir to the last Lord Stafford who died in 1913, the hall was eventually commandeered by the War Office as a training ground for the First World War soldiers and demolished shortly after that war.

At one time Costessey had six public houses The Falcon, Red Lion, White Hart, White Swan, Black Swan, and The Bush. There are now only two left, The Bush and the White Hart. (The Round Well public house is actually in New Costessey). The Round Well Obelisk outside the public house was built by French prisoners of war during the Napoleonic War about 1820. It was demolished and rebuilt in 1981.

The River Tud flows through Costessey Park and at one time crossed Longwater Lane by a ford over which pedestrians crossed by a footbridge. There were many footbridges built at various times over this ford from mid 1700s up until 1913 when the first road bridge was built. In 1969 a new road bridge was built over the ford which was then diverted under the new bridge.

The Catholic School was built by Sir George Jerningham in 1821 at his own expense. Teaching was by the Lancastrian Method in which more advanced pupils helped with the early teaching of the younger pupils. Roman Catholic Nuns were the main teachers at that time, but finally left the school in 1976 and the school then became known as St Augustines Primary School.

The Baptist School was built by Matthew Barber in 1837 and was demolished to make room for the car park to the new Baptist Hall in 1972. Teaching finished at the school after the 1870 Education Act brought in compulsory education.

The National School was built by the Rev. R. E. Hankinson in 1837 for forty children of C&E faith. Like the Baptist School it was closed down in 1870 when all village children were accommodated at the Roman Catholic School. The old National School building still exists tucked away up a narrow pathway against 86 The Street, and has been used for Toch.H, Church Council, Brownies and Children's Playgroups until it became rather derelict and dangerous and finally closed. It is now owned privately.

The Thatched Tudor Barn at the rear of the Butchers Shop was built in 1625. It was used at one time as the village abattoir and for cattle grazing on the adjacent field. This field is now being developed for new housing by Artision Dev. Company. Another Tudor Barn was built about 1688 against the Church, and was part of Church Farm. The old vicarage was part of the farm house but became derelict in the 1800s after which Eastwood Lodge and West Hill were used as temporary vicarages until the Rev. Hampson, in 1902, built the present day vicarage in Folgate Lane.

The first post office was opened up in 1850 in a front room of a private house situated at the front of the old White Hart. Letters came from Norwich by foot each morning. In 1898 a new post office was built in which a small telephone exchange switchboard was, in 1913, Installed. This remained until a new telephone exchange was built in 1932. By 1990 this post office was closed and the business transferred across the road to the enlarged Hart Stores.

Corn mills have been mentioned as being in Costessey on the River Wensum way back in the Domesday Book of 1087. In 1745 the mill on this site, being derelict, was rebuilt mainly in timber. By 1858 this corn mill had also been demolished and replaced by a five story brick and tile building. This mill was sold for modernisation in 1920 but, due to an oil engine fault, the mill was destroyed by fire in 1924 and never rebuilt. At the end of Windmill Lane was the Costessey post mill built in 1810 on the foundations of an earlier mill. It was advertised for sale in 1889 but not being sold was dismantled in 1902 leaving just the base roundhouse to be demolished in 1958.

The start up of the Costessey Brickworks is shrouded in antiquity, but perhaps, being sited on the Costessey Estate, it could have provided bricks for the first New Hall completed In 1565. It was enlarged in 1827 in order to provide the large number of bricks required for the building of the extension to the New Hall. At this time the brickyard was employing forty men and boys, but during the First World War production stopped and the brickyard was finally closed.

The last Lord Stafford died in 1913 and in 1918 the estate was broken up and sold. Many people, particularly from the tumble down areas of Norwich, flocked to Costessey and bought up plots of land for £5 per plot on which they dumped old railway carriages and assorted timber buildings. This somewhat ramshackled type of development soon became known as "China Town" and "The Back of the Beyond". The area became a mass of unmade dirt tracks, and it was not until after the Second World War, when most of the old buildings had been demolished, that Costessey and New Costessey became what it is today. Much more building has been done in both areas over the last year, particularly after the Costessey abattoir, in West End, was demolished in 1998.

St Edmund's Church was built about 1300 the Nave and Chancel during the 14th century and the Porch, with its elaborate flintwork, in the 15th century. At times the building has fallen into a poor state of repair particularly during the Penal Times 1558~1700, when an Act of Parliament enforced all Roman Catholics to abolish the celebration of Mass, and to attend their English Church, the failure of which could lead to imprisonment for life. At this time the local Catholic gentry allowed Costessey Church to fall into a very ruinous state which caused services to be abandoned, and they could not therefore attend their English Church. Over the years restoration work has been carried out, and ml 889 this included work on the roof. Repair work in the I 990s included the bell wheels and strengthening of the bell tower. In 1972 a second church was built in New Costessey and dedicated to St Helen.

The Roman Catholic Church was built by Lord Stafford, who also gave the land for the building, in 1830. This was due to the fact that the Chapel in Costessey Park was getting overcrowded with the increasing Catholic population in Costessey. It was in 1841, before the Church was finished. In 1871 Lord Stafford made over to the Rev Dr Husenbeth, as a personal free gift, the whole of the land and the church by which all became freehold property. One year later the Rev Dr Husenbeth died and all services, apart from funerals, were transferred back to the chapel in Costessey Park. The church, dedicated to Our Lady and St Walstan, was then closed and allowed to fall into a very dilapidated state with damp and dry rot in the structure. It was 1910 before Father Byrne brought the church back to full parochial use as it is today under the charge of Father Richard Wilson

Ernest G. Gage
Costessey.
Norwich. Norfolk

Produced in November 1999 for the Eastern Evening News WWW.

Hill Road and Hall Road New Costessey.

In 1840 the land on which Hill Road and Hall Road would eventually be built, was owned and occupied by Henry Harman. He was a very important farmer owning much land in both Costessey and New Costessey. At his death about 186Q the land was sold to Lord Stafford of Costessey Hall and rented out to various farmers, the last being Mr George Carr, a farmer of Costessey, whose name is perpetuated in Carr's Hill Wood off Folgate Lane, Costessey.

The last Lord Stafford died in 1913 and in November 1918. the Costessey Estate was broken up and this piece of land was offered for sale by auction. No buyer was forthcoming and, as Mr Carr had vacated it, the land was rented out to Messrs Dann and Son who held it until 1921 when the lease ran out.

The land was then offered for sale as building plots, and many people, particularly from the tumble-down areas of Norwich flocked to New Costessey and bought up building plots at £5 per plot. Local tradition tells of these buyers paying £5 for an acre of land, but I think that this a figment of somebody's imagination as no documentary evidence is available.

Once the plots were obtained, the new owners bought and dumped old railway carriages and built other assorted timber buildings on their plot of land. This somewhat ramshackled type of local development soon became known as "China Town" and "The Back of the Beyond" and of course, there was no local planning authority at that time. The area became a mass of unmade dirt tracts turning the area into an eyesore, hence the name "China Town" etc.

It was not until after the Second World War, when most of the original owners had departed, that demolition and planning order became the criterion for future development as we know it today.

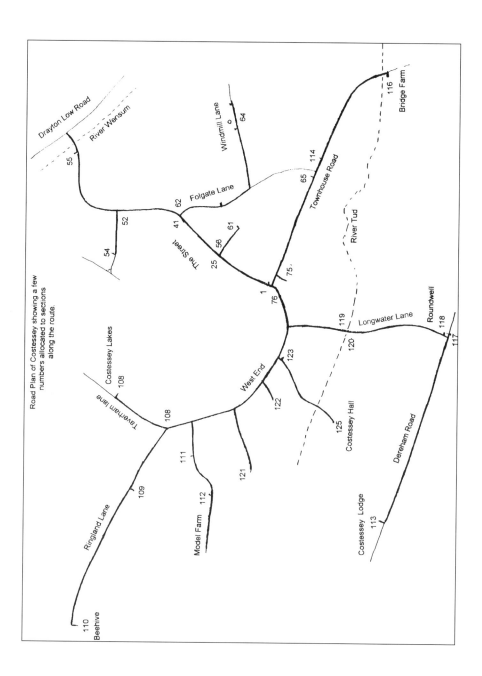

Road Plan of Costessey showing a few numbers allocated to sections along the route.

1

1880 Ordnance Survey Map

This extract from the 1880 Ordnance Survey map (plate 1a) covers the area surrounding the White Hart Plain, the start of the photographic tour of Costessey which is based mainly on old photographs.

At the bottom left corner is the Roman Catholic School (83) with Rose Cottage (84) above it on the extreme left. Further in to the right is the old Park Farm (80) with the old farm barns extending up to White Hart Plain. St Walstan's Roman Catholic Church (75) is at the bottom right, and above, on the opposite side of Townhouse Road, is the Old Forge (73). To the left of this is the very first Costessey Post Office (77) and just above it is the Old White Hart (76). Across the road to the left is the Old Blacksmith's Shop and what is now the present day Post Office (78). Next to the old White Hart is Hart House (3) and just above it stands the old Baker's Shop (4). Other buildings can be easily identified from the following photographs such as the butcher's shop and Glen Cottage (plate 11b) at the top right corner.

The aerial photograph (plate 1b) also covers the area surrounding the White Hart Plain and shows, in the foreground, the barns of Park Farm abattoir (80). Just above the barns is a pair of semi-detached cottages which were built on the site of an old marl pit after it had been filled in and levelled about 1906. Along the street are buildings mentioned in sections 3 to 5, and slightly further on and set back from the roadway is the Baptist Chapel (8). The building at the road edge just to the left of the chapel is the old Baptist School, now demolished together with the row of cottages (5).

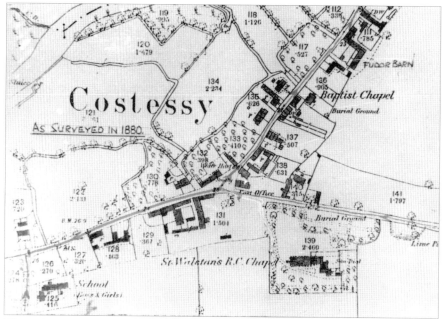

Plate 1a   Year 1880

Plate 1b   Year 1951

3

2
Street Scene with Old White Hart
T.52

This photograph, taken in about 1900, shows a view looking northwards up the street. On the right is the old White Hart, the entrance to which is seen in this old photograph. On the opposite side of the street is the old orchard belonging to John Spaul, a well known village blacksmith at that time, who worked in the nearby blacksmith's shop (plate 78a). After his death his wife sold the property to the Costessey Estate. At the 1918 Estate sale the property was bought by Frederick Gunton who was the tenant of the blacksmith's shop and village stores (78). In 1960, the orchard was sold for building, and all the property seen along the street apart from the old baker's shop (plate 4b) have now been demolished.

Plate 2   *Year 1900*

4

3

Street Scene with Hart House – T. 171

On the extreme right is part of the old White Hart with a cartway entrance between the public house and the adjacent cottage, against which a small boy is standing. This building was named as Hart House in the 1918 sale of Costessey Estate. In 1890 the tenant was George Flatman, the stables at the rear being used for his ponies and traps. He was still living here in 1918 and was running a pony and trap transport service. Like other transport services in Costessey, he was forced off the road by the newly formed United Bus Service in about 1925. Further along the street is Burnett's bakery and grocery shop (4) which Ernest Burnett opened up in about 1920, and next to it is the gable end of a row of cottages (5).

Opposite and a little further on is the outline of a building reputed to have been the Old White Swan public house built at the turn of the 19th century. The publican, John Miller, was running this public house and the White Hart at the same time. George Durrant became the owner of the White Swan in 1857 and then sold it to the Rev. James Evans (at Costessey from 1843 to 1896) perhaps for his own accommodation as there was no vicarage as such at that time. The old building was demolished by a local builder who then built Kent House, 13 The Street, on the cleared site.

Plate 3

Year 1925

4
Old Bakery Shop
6 The Street
T.190

The first mention of this old property is on the 6th of August 1669 when Thomas Barker succeeded to it by the will of his mother, Judith Barker. In 1842 it was owned by Mary Hastings Spaul and, on her death, her daughter, Sarah, succeeded. She had married Henry Wilde, a market gardener, but they became bankrupt and had to sell the property. Sarah is seen in this photograph standing outside the property with her husband standing against the wall in the background. Samuel Garerd, a Norwich solicitor, became the next owner until he sold out to Ernest Burnett.

A shop was then constructed extending from the front of the building almost to the road edge, with Ernest Burnett using the rear of the building as his accommodation. He died in 1927 at the age of 47, leaving the business to be carried on by his widow, Emma Burnett, who kept up the bakery until closing it in 1937, and the shop until 1945 when she retired. Her eldest daughter, Gladys, then took over the shop until 1959 when she retired, selling the shop and property to Mr Chatten, who, in 1961, sold out to Mr Moss. He built up a good grocery business which he later rented to Mr Briggs. Eventually Mr Briggs moved to Cromer and the shop was let to another grocer, but the business failed and the shop was closed.

In 1976, Mr Moss sold out to Alan Fairweather, a local builder, who let out the shop to various tenants, including a nearly new clothes shop, an audio cassette shop and a second-hand furniture shop, which later on moved to premises further up the street (15). The shop was then sold to Mr and Mrs Wells who opened up a business selling nearly new children's clothes and equipment. They, however, closed it down in June 1995 and put the shop on the market for sale but, as it remained unsold for over two years, have now demolished the frontage of the shop and reconstructed it as a private residence.

Plate 4a   *Year 1884*

Plate 4b   *Year 1925*

Plate 4c   *Year 1995*

5
Street Scene with four old Cottages
The Street
T.29 and T.567

In the foreground on the left are the four old cottages that were demolished in the 1970s. The records of this site go back to 1696 when John Graver, a blacksmith, bought the only cottage that stood on this site. Christmas Robert Sidney bought it in 1829, demolished it, and then built the two cottages that are seen against the telephone pole.

The 1840 Tithe Award lists John Sidney as the owner with John White as one of the occupiers. Another occupier was William Doggett, called Stumpy Doggett because of his wooden leg. He was a shoemaker and also the village lamplighter, lighting the one lamp that stood on White Hart Plain (76).

The additional two cottages, part of which is seen in the near foreground, were built by William Blomfield, a Norwich shopkeeper, and in 1840 the listed occupiers were William Neville and Thomas Sissens. Another occupier was Matthew Breeze, at one time the Parish Clerk. In 1903, these cottages were sold to Charles Clarke, a corn merchant of Norwich, for an annuity which Mrs Grubb, the previous owner, enjoyed for many years.

These four cottages were condemned in the 1960s and finally demolished to clear the site for a new Baptist Hall (plate 8). In the distance on the left are the old cottages (3), and on the right foreground is part of the Thatched Cottage (6). The old Baptist School (8) stood at the near end of the old cottages seen on the extreme left.

Plate 5

Year 1951

6 (L)
Thatched Cottage
11 The Street
T.28

The first known owner of this property was Robert Graver, a blacksmith, who acquired the property in 1686. By 1812 it had become the property of Richard and Elizabeth Bond. At the time of the 1840 Tithe Award the premises had two tenants, Thomas Spaul and William Skipper, known as Hookey Skipper. It was said locally that he was a general dealer and had a donkey and a horse and cart. He would sell chickens to his customers and later that night would go round and steal them back to be sold again the next day. He met an untimely end on Ringland Hills with his horse and cart on top of him.

At the rear of the building was a half-acre garden used as an orchard and hop growing area. The property was eventually sold to the Costessey Estate in 1856 and, at the time of the 1918 Costessey Estate sale, the tenants were listed as Sergeant Frost and Mr Spaul paying a total rent of £8.5.0. per annum. The property was sold to a London speculator, R.H.Tebb, for £160, and at this time was divided into two dwellings with a single central entrance lobby, each having two rooms downstairs and one room upstairs with an attic window in the gable-ends. The central chimney stack is original but the fireplaces are of later construction. The roof timbers appear to be original with butt purlins and former collars.

The property has long since been converted into a single storey dwelling and Miss Irene M. Hodgson lived here for many years until her death in December 1993 at over 90 years of age, a death perhaps hastened by a burglary. Much antique furniture was stolen whilst she was still in the cottage.

The cottage is now being completely renovated by the new owner, Mr Derek Davies, who acquired the property after selling Crete Lodge (plate 112a).

Plate 6

7

Thatched Cottages
15 The Street
T.170

The first known owner of these two cottages was Henry Ives who sold them to John Liddelow for £40 in 1736. John Harman bought them in 1851 and sold them to the Costessey Estate in 1873. They were bought by R.H.Tebb at the 1918 sale of the Costessey Estate. The last tenants were Tom Boughthorpe and Harry Elvin. One Sunday morning Tom's daughter was drying clothes against the open fire when a sudden draught of air forced the clothes up the chimney which caught fire and set light to the thatched roof. Both cottages were destroyed and, as no other home was available for Tom Boughthorpe, they had to go into Bowthorpe Poor Law Institution, (now the West Norwich Hospital).

In 1932, the derelict site was acquired by the General Post Office for a new telephone exchange as the switchboard in the old post office (77) was over-subscribed. This new telephone exchange had accommodation for a live-in operator who would have to get up to answer late night or early morning calls. When a modern telephone exchange was built in New Costessey in the 1960s, this old building was converted into private property and sold.

Plate 7   *Year 1918*

8
Baptist Chapel and School Room
The Street
T.157

The Manorial Records of 29th July 1822 report that 'Matthew Barker surrendered for the sum of £4, all that piece of land upon which a chapel for Divine Worship has lately been built with a burial ground at the rear'. Later, in 1837, Matthew Barker bought a small piece of land from the adjacent owner, W. Blomfield, for £12 on which to build a School Room (5). This was called the British School Room and became part of the chapel land.

John Ivory was one of the first teachers, to be followed by Ellen Skoyles, and then Miss Martha Skoyles. Like the National School further along the street (27), it was most probably closed after the 1870 Education Act which brought in compulsory education. The school room continued to be used as a Sunday School and Baptist Hall in which many groups held their activities. During the Second World War the hall was used as the headquarters of the Home Guard.

During the late 1950s a new hall was planned which required two of the adjacent four cottages to be purchased (5). The new hall was eventually built and opened on 24th May 1969, but the construction of the full car park had to wait until 1972 when the old school hall was finally demolished with the adjacent cottages. The new Baptist Hall is now used extensively by many local groups for various activities.

Plate 8

9
Cottage and Garden, 24 The Street
T. 27

The 1840 Tithe Award describes this property as two cottages giving Matthew Barker as the owner, with John Spaul and John Denny as the tenants. His son, Robert, succeeded and, on his death in 1864, it was inherited by John Goldsmith, a shop- keeper. On his death in 1883 his executors sold out to the Costessey Estate.

One of the first Estate tenants was George Burnett, a miller's waggoner employed by John Culley of Costessey Mill (53). George Burnett started up as a corn chandler in this shop in about 1890, and died in 1915. However, in 1912, Ernest Burnett had taken over the shop and turned it into a bakery business. Lord Stafford, the owner of the property, died in 1913 and the sale of all Estate property was planned. This took place in November 1918 when the property was listed as House, Bakery, Shop and land, and occupied by Ernest Burnett. He then decided to buy some property further up the street and to transfer his business there (4). At the Estate sale the property was withdrawn at £360.

The next owner of the property was Frederick John Ottaway. He added a hardware store in what was the old baker's shop and started up an oil round taking a large tank of paraffin on the back of his truck, and built up a successful business. He died in 1944 at the age of 64 and was succeeded by his son, Thomas Frederick Ottaway. His wife, Ethel, took over the running of the shop and it was said that she had some difficulty in getting Fred out on the rounds with his paraffin tank and hardware goods. He died in 1978 at the age of 63, and was described in his funeral records as a labourer employed at Laurence Scott and Electromotors of Norwich. After his death, his widow, Ethel, sold the property to David and Elizabeth Tosh.

Plate 9

10 (L)
Thatched Tudor Barn, 28 The Street
T.30

Situated at the rear of the butcher's shop is an old Tudor barn built in 1625, which predates the church Tithe Barn of 1688. It has a similar roof design although not so intricately constructed. The first known owner was Phillip Vincent of Marlingford, who also owned the adjacent 12 acre field.

Matthew Barker, having bought the property in 1811 (8), sold the barn and the 12 acre field to William Banham in 1837. He had the adjacent butcher's business which he retained for the next twenty- five years, after which he sold the whole of the property to the Costessey Estate (11). He remained as tenant to be followed after his death by William Cannell, who bought the property after the 1918 sale of the Costessey Estate. At this time the barn was used as an abattoir and for livestock when the field was used for cattle grazing. Mr Barnes was the head slaughterer for Mr Cannell and Bert Gunton, one of five sons brought up in the very small cottage, extreme left (plate

Plate 10   *Year 1951*

18

12), was the assistant slaughterer. However, it was understood that personal difficulties overcame him and after attempting drowning in the nearby River Wensum, he returned to the abattoir where he then shot himself.

The Tudor Barn remained in the Cannell family until the death of Herbert Cannell in 1954 after which it was sold, together with the 12 acre field, to Miss Amy Bates of Beech Cottage (71). She renovated the barn and had it re-thatched before letting it to Mr Moss (4). He was followed by Messrs Balding and Masters, musical instrument repairers, but their business failed and the barn was next hired by Gosden, an office management business, which then bought the barn from Miss Bates. This business also failed and went into receivership. The barn was then sold in March 1992 to Mr Steven Hunter who makes and repairs furniture to individual order. The 12 acre field was retained by Miss Bates who had contracted with Birds Eye Foods to supply them with any vegetable requirements and, with the help of Miss Margery Lewis, the land became very profitable.

Planning permission was sought in 1964 for the 12 acre field but was refused. It has since been granted on appeal and the field is being developed for housing. Two of the roads, Hinshalwood Way and Kirklands, are named after a Scottish doctor who served the community for many years.

Plate 10a   *Year 1955*

11
Butcher's Shop, 30 The Street
T.30

Like the Tudor Barn (10) this shop was also sold to the Costessey Estate in 1862. It was bought by William Cannell (plate 11a) at the 1918 sale of the Estate for £1,175. He could neither read nor write and was said to be very tight with his money. He died in 1927 leaving a reputed total of £68,000, a great amount of money at that time. His son, Herbert, who was the occupier of the shop at the time of the Estate sale became the owner of the property including the Tudor Barn.

After the death of Herbert Cannell in 1954, the property was inherited by his wife, who sold the Tudor Barn and the 12 acre field to Miss Amy Bates (10). The house and butcher's shop was sold to Frederick Standing who remained in business until 1958 when he sold out to Stanley Pickering. He continued running the business until bad health forced him to retire

Plate 11a   *Year 1900*

Plate 11b   *Year 1914*

Plate 11c   *Year 1951*

in 1981. His son, Bryan, took over and greatly improved the shop layout. He achieved the distinction of being elected 'Butcher of the Year' in the 1987 National Show.

Adjacent to the north end of the butcher's house, stood an old Tudor cottage (plate 11b) which was first mentioned in Manorial Records of 1697. It was eventually sold in 1909 to William Cannell, the Estate tenant of the butcher's shop at that time.

During the Second World War part of this old cottage was used by the Air Raid Wardens for their headquarters and equipment. By 1954, when Herbert Cannell died, this old Tudor cottage (plate 11c) had greatly deteriorated and by 1960 the three tenants had been rehoused. The property was then bought by William Smith for demolition.

In 1971 the property was still listed under the name of Glen Cottage T.566, in the register prepared by the Department of the Environment (1) for preservation, and was described as a 17th century building, but, by this time, it had long since been demolished and the site developed.

Plate 11d

12

Two Pairs of Semi-detached Cottages, 36 - 42 The Street – T.565

These old cottages, set back from The Street and with very long front gardens, were owned by John Sidney in 1840 together with the now demolished Glen Cottage. These cottages were also sold to William Cannell in 1909 (11). When Herbert Cannell became the owner in 1927, the tenant in 42 The Street was Mrs Gunton who managed to bring up five sons in this very small house (10).

As the properties became empty, William Cannell took the opportunity to sell them.When Mrs Gunton vacated 42 The Street it was sold to Mr George Cannell, who remained living here until his death at the age of 91 in 1997. He had been a very reliable source of information for this record.

In 1970 Mrs Doggett who lived next door to Mr Cannell found Mrs Boltham, a church organist for 24 years, dead on the floor of 38 The Street, having been overcome by smoke from her cottage fire. Mrs Doggett was moved into care in 1995, and her cottage sold to Bunn Builders for renovation and resale. The adjacent cottages, 36-38 The Street, are also being renovated by the new owners.

Plate 12

13
Street Scene, The Street

This view (13a) is part of the Street looking north from the butcher's shop (10). On the left can be seen the old Central Stores (15). On the right hand side can be seen the corner of the old Tudor cottage, Glen View (11). Next along the street is a pair of semi-detached cottages, now 44-46 The Street. These were built by James Howell in 1829 and the Tithe Award T.188 lists him as the owner, with the tenants being Ann Morday and Charles Boyle. In 1871, Robert Burton of Norwich purchased them and after his death in 1899 they went to his son, Robert. Sometime between the two World Wars the property was bought by a Mr Taylor who lived here until his death in 1950, and his widow remained here until her death in the 1960s, with Robert Goodwin occupying the adjacent cottage. Nicholas Smith bought what is now 46 The Street in 1991, whilst Paul Walker acquired 44 The Street in 1995.

Next along the street and built right up to the road edge is a pair of very small semi- detached cottages. The 1840 Tithe Award T.187 lists James Howell as the owner with Philip Frost and Thomas Sporle as tenants. This building became unfit for human habitation and was used only as a store by John Harman, a local farmer (plate 115) and (plate 124). It has long since been demolished but is seen in the foreground on plate 13b.

Between the two buildings just mentioned can be seen the gable-end of a cottage T.160. This was built about 1895 on the site of a row of three old cottages and a shop and known as Birds Yard, the first known owner being William Smith who acquired them in 1685. In1806 they came into the Savage family who used the shop for their harness making business until they moved to West End (95). In 1893 Birds Yard was sold to the solicitors for Costessey Estate (Preface) and then demolished, and by 1895 had been replaced by the building now 50 The Street, the first occupier being Albert Palmer, a carpenter and builder (102). Eventually William Barnes, a butcher, became the occupier and his widow remained here until her death in1966. John Crickmore bought this property in 1991 but, by the end of 1996, it was again up for sale and has been sold to Jonathan Miller, a painter and decorator.

Plate 13a   *Year 1910*

Plate 13b   *Year 1910*

Plate 13c   *Year 1995*

25

14
Row of Cottages, 45 - 49 The Street
T.145, T.154, T.172 and T.184

Five of the old cottages seen in this row have already been demolished. The old cottage on the extreme left with the dormer window was known as Gooseholme and records go back to 1704 when Richard Woodcock sold it to John and Mary Skipper. It then passed through many other owners and occupiers before demolition.

In August 1912 the nearby River Wensum overflowed its banks. Flood water came up and entered the rear door and went out via the front door into the street. Mrs Shickle, the occupier at the time (plate 14b), is seen helping it on its way. The cottages adjacent to Gooseholme are listed in the 1840 Tithe Award as being owned by Peter Finch, John Culley, and Robert Humphrey, with tenants Thomas Adcock, James Edwards, Peter Savage and John Sparkes.

In June 1856 the archway cottage was sold to William Edwards who, with his wife Maria, set up a laundry business in the room over the archway entrance to the meadow at the rear. A hoist protruded through the top front window and by means of pulley and tackle, baskets of laundry were raised to this upper room. William Edwards died in 1881 but his wife carried on for a few years until she retired. The laundry was then taken over by two sisters, the Misses Sissens, but when they retired the business was closed.

Plate 14a
Year 1914

26

By 1930 these old buildings were almost derelict but were made habitable and used for Second World War evacuees. After the war most were demolished, but in 1945 Edmund Seaman bought the old archway cottage and the adjoining cottage at the rear. The two remaining cottages, now 47 - 49 The Street, were therefore saved from demolition, with Julie Greenwood buying 47 in1987 and William Stone acquiring 49 in 1956. Both of these properties became vacant in 1997 when Julie Greenwood moved out and William Stone died. Number 47 is now rented out whilst number 49 has been sold to Graham Perry, a retired police officer, for renovation and occupation.

Plate 14b   *Year 1912*

The horse drawn waggon seen on the extreme right is a flour waggon from Costessey Mill (plate 53c).

Plate 14c
Year 1993

27

15

Central Stores and Bakery, 51 The Street
T.168

The 1840 Tithe Award describes this property as bake office and yard, and lists Peter Finch as the owner with James Edwards as the occupier and baker. By 1883 John Pratt (plate 15a) had bought it and carried on the bakery until his death in 1898 at 54 years of age when he was succeeded by his wife, Maria. John Pratt died intestate which caused his wife, Maria, to attend the Costessey Manorial Court in July 1899 by virtue of the Intestates Estates Act of 1890. She successfully obtained tenancy of her late husband's property which otherwise would have been seized by the bailiff on behalf of Lord Stafford.

Maria Pratt died in 1900 and in her will bequeathed her property to such persons as John William Ottaway, her uncle, should appoint and, in default, the property was to go to her nephew, Ernest Fulcher Ottaway. Default there was, and it was only through the diligence of John Lyons (97), a well known Costessey man who located Ernest Ottaway and brought him, just in time, to the Manorial Court in July 1901, that the bailiff was prevented, once again, from seizing the property for Lord Stafford after the Court's third and final proclamation for such persons to appear.

After taking possession of the old bake office property Ernest Ottaway demolished it and in its place built a modern house and shop with a bakery at the rear, all of which were extended later on to make a much larger shop (plate 15b). During his short lifetime in Costessey, from 1901 to 1920 when

Plate 15a   *Year 1886*

28

he died at 45 years of age, he took great interest in photography, providing some of the old photographs used in this record. His widow carried on the business with the help of her son, Norman, but after his death the bakery and shop was closed.

The shop premises which are now owned by Kevin Shortis of Costessey House (50) have since been occupied by various business concerns, but have now been taken over by Abel's secondhand furniture store which had previously been located in the old bakery and grocer's shop, further down the street (4).

Plate 15b   *Year 1918*

Plate 15c   *Year 1994*

16
The Bush Public House, The Street
T.557

The first known owner of The Bush public house was Robert Armes who died in 1642, but by 1854 Lucy Steward became the owner, with John Taylor, a watchmaker and Parish Clerk, being the listed tenant in 1864. In 1877 it went to Peter Finch who died in 1880. He left it in half shares to Elizabeth Brightwell and H.T.S. Patteson who, in 1883, sold the adjoining bakehouse and cottage to John Pratt (15). Robert Anderson was the landlord when Steward and Patteson was legally formed as a company in 1895 (plate 16a). He was followed by Charles Millar, Joseph Tilletson, Horace Sexton and Bertie Blogg, by which time in the early 1930s The Bush had been rebuilt.

In 1963 Steward and Patteson was taken over by Watney Mann, who were merged with Grand Metropolitan in 1971. They were followed by Phoenix Inns Ltd, whose tenant landlords stay for only short periods before moving out. A little further on just past The Bush can be seen the gable-end of Ambreys and Grymes (17).

Plate 16a   *Year 1914*

Plate 16b

Plate 16c

17
Ambreys and Grymes
T.577

The site on which these old cottages stood, just north of The Bush (plates 16a 17), was owned by John Wilson who died in 1683. His son, John, inherited it with his widow succeeding in1714. John Taylor, who was the occupier of the adjacent public house, bought these cottages in1838. He died in 1864 when his wife, Joanna, succeeded. Caius Spaul, a tailor and postmaster of Costessey (77), took possession in 1885 and ten years later Arthur Roberts, a wheelwright, bought them. He sold them to Steward and Patteson in about 1913, but they were demolished by the new owners of The Bush in the 1970s to provide additional car parking space.

According to Tithe Award T.577, another small building named Goodales was joined or adjacent to Ambreys and Grymes, but although shown on the 1840 Tithe sketch map, it is not shown on the 1880 Ordnance Survey map, so must have been demolished before 1880.

Plate 17   *Year 1930*

18 (L)
Riverside House, 63 The Street
T.20

The first mention of this very old Tudor house was in the Manorial Records of January 1779 when Eldon Money, a Costessey farmer and land owner, bought it from the executors of Nockhold Thompson. Eldon Money sold it to William Carr in 1782 and, in 1795 whilst it was in Carr's ownership, the Rev.Wilkes, then living in Costessey, held the first recorded Baptist service in one of the rooms (8).

James Linall bought it in 1853 at which time the small adjoining cottage was occupied by Hannah Scott who, until about 1860, used to drive cows to the eastern common along what is now known as Townhouse Road. There she acted as gatekeeper to allow travellers through, whilst confining the cows to the common. James Linall died in 1866 and his daughter sold the property to Charles Clarke for an annuity which she enjoyed for many years (5).

Plate 18a

Year 1951

33

Other occupiers of Riverside House were the ancestors of George Cannell (12) whose father was born in Hannah Scott's small cottage, whilst his great grandfather occupied the main adjoining house. G.W. Thompson of Costessey Mill (53) was also an occupier until the mill was sold in 1920. The property was later sold to Ernest Gowing and his widow lived here until her death in 1992, after which it was sold to Anthony and Linda Holmes, who also own Inglenook next door (23).

Col. Glendenning, an authority on Tudor houses, dated this property back to 1600 and pointed out that one room had a good example of Queen Anne wall panelling. He said the property appeared to have been built by someone with more refined tastes than those of the average yeoman. He identified the small annexe, Hannah Scott's cottage, as a possible brewhouse for the early occupants of Riverside House. This cottage is seen at the further gable end of the main house.

Plate 18b   *Year 1993*

34

19

Small Cottage Opposite The Bush P.H.
56 The Street
T.224

The first known owner of this small cottage was Robert Gimont who sold it to Philip Vincent in 1697. James Laws bought it in 1833 for £188, but this also included the land which covered a larger area than it does today. He died in 1851 and his widow sold it to the Costessey Estate in 1857 for £200, including the land.

At the 1918 Costessey Estate sale, the cottage, which was in the occupation of Mr J. Webb at a rental of £7 per annum, was bought by E.J. Hardingham for £105.Herbert Day occupied it in 1961 but after he left in the same year, the property remained empty and by 1965 was almost derelict. It was completely renovated and in 1968 Mr E. Fenwick (76) sold Holmwood (23) and moved into this cottage staying for a number of years until it was sold to Brian Duffield, an insurance executive, in 1983.

Plate 19

20
Cottages opposite
The Bush North Car Park
58, 60 and 62 The Street
T. 569

The first known owner of these cottages was John Gunton who acquired them in 1660 and sold them to Mary Wilson in 1698. She later became Mary Skipper and in 1717 the property was in the name of John and Mary Skipper (21). By 1798 they were in the possession of William Neal who built an extra cottage on to the north end of the cottages making three cottages in this row. It is probable that he raised the roof of the pair of old cottages to line up with the new cottage being built. Observation of the south gable-end wall will show the tumbling brickwork of the original roof line. Because of the soft nature of Norfolk red bricks, a method of forming a sound coping to a gable-end wall was to lay bricks at right angles to the gable-end coping to form a series of triangles. This is known as 'tumbling'. The Flemish immigrants who settled in this area in the 15th century brought with them their skills of brickmaking, bonding and tumbling.

In 1812 the three cottages were sold to John Blake, a Norwich solicitor.They remained in the Blake family until1885 when Steven Hubbard bought them and in 1901 sold them to Joseph Coverdale, the Estate Agent at Costessey Hall.

Katherine Gunton bought them in 1912 and, although she died in 1919, her husband, William, retained them until his death in 1944. A year later his two daughters, Agnes and Selina, sold them to Hilton Blake, owner of the abattoir (80). Many tenants have occupied these cottages including well-known names of the past such as John Palmer, Fred Arthurton, George Barley, Albert White, Paul Ribbons, Ann Futter, Edward Futter and Mary Skipper.

Miss Olive Crane occupied number 58 The Street and when it became empty, Hilton Blake sold it to David Jordan, and when Elsie Greenacre

Plate 20

moved from number 60 this was then sold to Gavin Willis. After he had renovated it he sold it in 1994 to Karen Cordell. Hilton Blake had previously sold number 62 to Mr Frost in about 1957, but after his death in about 1980, the property was sold to Brian Freeman who has renovated it, exposing rare old oak beams which had been covered with plaster.

21

The Old Guildhouse
and Blacksmith's Shop
64 - 66 The Street
T.285

This is one of the most interesting properties in Costessey as it was, in earlier times, the Old Guildhouse, for which the earliest mention was in 1479 when William Breyden of Costessey left 'one comb of barley to the light called sowlmy at ye Gylhows'. The next mention is in 1717 at the Manorial Court when John Skipper obtained possession of the then two cottages (20) to the south of the Guildhouse.

Amongst the records of the Costessey Hall Estate are frequent mentions of the Guildhouse farm and one stated that the rent of £7.16s would be better at £18 per annum. The 1840 Tithe Award gives Thomas Bealey, a native of East Dereham, as the occupier of what was referred to as a 'House, Shop and Garden'. He had a shop in the house and was a wheelwright. The brick and flint infill near the south gable-end would most probably have been the entrance to the shop.

William Gooderson from Norwich, a wheelwright and blacksmith, became the occupier in the 1880s with his son, William, carrying on the business until about 1900 when Arthur Roberts, also a wheelwright, became the occupier. His son, Thomas, followed him but only as a blacksmith and he and his wife were the occupiers at the time of the 1918 Costessey Estate sale when the property was withdrawn at £140. According to Kelly's Directory of 1929, Thomas Roberts was still occupying the premises and was also recorded as a 'rag and bone' merchant.

The old south gable-end wall is medieval, containing 15th century brickwork and flintwork. The roof line of this gable-end also contains a perfect example of Flemish coping known as 'tumbling' (20). The original house and shop at this south end has part of a wall 20 inches thick and was constructed possibly in the 18th century out of rubble acquired from the part demolition of the medieval building, although the street wall is part of the original house.

Plate 21   *Year 1951*

Alan Leggett acquired the property and, after it became vacant, he demolished the north gable-end wall and extended the building towards the north. This extension is easily recognised by its modern construction. The premises were then divided into two dwellings, and, in 1961, the occupiers were Frank Reynolds and Leonard Barnard. Alan Leggett then sold the property with the north end extension to Judith Wiseman who, in 1994, sold it to Ray Crook. The adjoining cottage with the original south gable-end wall is owned by Glenis Crowe and let to tenants.

Further on, just past the old Guildhouse and built almost on to the road edge, is a small single-storey building. This was the first purpose-built Methodist Chapel (22) in Costessey and was opened in 1886.

22
Cottages and Methodist Chapel
68, 70 and 72 The Street
T.568

The first mention of this property was in 1677 when, at a Manorial Court, John Hudson acquired it from the surrender of Rodger Blyth. In 1875 William Churchyard arrived in Costessey and acquired not only this property but also the adjoining property (26) which, in 1862, had accommodation for the first Methodist chapel in Costessey. Previous to this the Methodists used to hold some of their meetings in a granary which has long since been demolished. In this granary chapel candles were used and small boys would often blow these out during prayers. We do know that the Methodists used the old barn (41) for their anniversaries, so perhaps the granary was part of this old barn.

William Churchyard then proceeded to build up a very successful business as a baker, grocer and general stores in the adjoining property (26) and to such an extent that the accommodation used as a Methodist chapel was required for this increasing bakery business. He then used the front of his adjoining site and, in1886, constructed the first purpose-built Methodist Chapel. The first sermon was preached in it by the Rev. J. Percival, and at this time a Mr H. Bumphrey (64) was the leader. 'The Norwich Methodist Magazine' of December 1937 stated in their historical report that the old chapel accommodation in the adjoining property was then used as a bake office.

Joseph Morter acquired the property in 1935 and then converted the two north end cottages into one dwelling, making what had been three cottages into two. He also demolished the small barn, and occupied what is now 68 The Street with Mr and Mrs Smith occupying 70 The Street, next door. Mrs Smith went round the village with a pony and cart selling fish which she had bought from the Norwich Fish Market.

Col.Glendenning (mentioned earlier) inspected these two cottages in 1951 and said that 68 The Street contained a Henry VIII beam and the next door property contained a beam with a different moulding, from Queen Elizabeth's time. He dated the original timber buildings as being approximately 16th century.

40

Plate 22   *Year 1993*

Joseph Morter died in 1964, but the property remained in the Morter family until 1987 when 68 The Street was sold to David Vince. Mr and Mrs Jack Spence acquired 70 The Street and renovated it exposing several very old beams. It is now owned by Deborah Boyd. The Methodist chapel continued in use until the mid 1960s when a new chapel was built in Norwich Road, New Costessey, and the old now redundant chapel was converted into private accommodation and sold to Mrs D.M. Ashmore. She died in 1987 and it was bought by Nigel and Lisa Dinsdale.

23

Inglenook and Holmwood
67 and 69 The Street
T.151

The first known owner of Holmwood was George Betts who sold it to Henry Negus in 1790. The 1840 Tithe Award mentions a pair of semi-detached cottages and a smaller cottage on this site and in 1890 they were acquired by George Cannell. He moved into one of the semi-detached cottages whilst his son, Charles, occupied the next door north-side cottage both having just moved from Riverside House (18). It was in this north-side cottage that George Cannell (12) was born in 1905, with his father, Charles Cannell, working the ground as a market gardener and smallholder. He died in 1922 and the property was sold to H. C. Greengrass, a builder, for £100. He turned the pair of semi-detached cottages into one modern dwelling, now known as Holmwood, 69 The Street, and sold it to Mr Crosskill of Norwich for £580. Mrs Baker occupied it for several years but, after she left, Mr E. Fenwick, who had just retired from the tenancy of the White Hart (76), bought the property. He remained here until 1968 when he moved into a small cottage (19) after selling Holmwood to Dr R. Hull.

After carrying out the work on the pair of semi-detached cottages Mr Greengrass then demolished the other small building which had long been used as a store, and built a house for his son. This property is now known as Inglenook, 67 The Street. Later on Mr Greengrass (junior) was followed by Mr and Mrs Russell who remained here for several years. In 1984 it was sold by auction to Anthony and Linda Holmes who, in 1994, acquired the adjacent property, Riverside House (18).

Plate 23 – 'Holmwood'

24

Shop and Bakehouse
75 The Street
T.240

Four old cottages were standing on this site when John Hods had it in 1811, but by 1905 the cottages were reported as being very dangerous and were demolished. Alan Leggett acquired the site and built a shop with a bakehouse at the rear. He then opened the shop as a grocery and was still in business here when he bought the next-door property, Riverside (25). He later sold the shop and bakery to Ashworth, Bakers and Caterers of Norwich, who ran the shop under a local manageress. After the death of Mr Ashworth, his son and daughter-in-law took over the shop. They were not successful and soon had to close down. Mr Rosier acquired the business and proved a very successful grocer but for health reasons had to sell the business. Mr Kenneth Bingham acquired it but, due to the health of Mrs Bingham, the business was sold to Mr and Mrs Claridge. They were not successful and the shop was closed.

The property was then sold to a property agent who rented it out to Kirby Cleaners, and then to Alex Cook, a mobile telephone company. They stayed for only a short period of time, and the property was sold to Abbs and Oxborrow of Little Ellingham, Norfolk. They sold it in 1993 to Brian Sharples, a Swaffham solicitor, but the shop remained empty until May 1995 when Van Kleets, a children's clothes business, took it over on a one year lease. The lease was not renewed and the shop is still vacant.

Plate 24   *Year 1994*

25
Riverside, 79 The Street
T.238

The first mention of this old property is in 1771 when John White sold it to James Hods. It was then a small farm with associated barns and was eventually bought by Joseph Wills, a speculator from Sheringham, in about 1900. He had the old farm house and barns demolished and the present day large residence built, with Dr Lichtenberg taking up residence. Hugh J. Boswell, a Norwich stockbroker, followed and he improved and extended the house and garden. He died in 1933 when his neighbour, Alan Leggett, a grocer owning the adjacent shop (24), bought it and rented it to Mr W. H. Middleton, a Costessey Parish Councillor.

During the Second World War, 1939-45, part of the house was used by the Forehoe and Henstead Rural District Council as a Ministry of Food Office, and food ration books were issued from here Mr Middleton still remaining as tenant. In 1960, the property was sold to Dr Murphy, mainly for him to acquire enough land to provide a side entrance for motor vehicles to his adjoining property, St Mary's (33). Mr Middleton remained as tenant until 1974 when Dr Murphy sold the house and the remaining part of the land to Mr Larkins, a dental surgeon. He carried on his dental practice in the small annexe at the southern end of the main residence until 1968, when he became very depressed and, unfortunately, severely injured himself. The property was then sold to Mr Bellamy, a chief claims manager for Norwich Union.

He sold out in 1976 to Norman Brooks, a local weather recorder, who provided weather records and data to the 'Eastern Daily Press' and associated papers. He was an enthusiastic collector of wartime memorabilia, an interest he has maintained since he moved to France in 1993. He now has a connection with 'La Maison Blanche' an hotel at Mailly, used by the Germans during the 1940-44 occupation of France and which contains many pictures and mementoes of both world wars. Riverside was then sold to David Porteous who has carried out a large scale renovation of the building, particularly to the street facing wall where all old cement rendering was removed, exposing the original red brickwork of the 1900 period.

Plate 25

26
Warehouse, Shop and Bakery
74, 76 and 78 The Street
T.9

The earliest known owner of Fernley (plate 26b), now 76 The Street, was Lockyer Byer who, in 1709, left it to his son, James. In 1810 James Rampling bought it and remained as owner until 1839 when he sold it to James Arthurton. He ran a small shop here and also acted as an estate agent and school master teaching at the National School (27). The 1840 Tithe Award lists James Arthurton as the owner of this site which comprised four small cottages with gardens, the occupiers being James Arthurton, Thomas Newton, Edmund Barley and Frances Barley. In 1849 James Arthurton sold out to John Whisker, a Bawburgh shop keeper, but after only six years trading he sold out to Elizabeth Davy of Norwich.

In 1875 William Churchyard bought the property from her and it is more than probable that he demolished the old cottages when he extended the front of Fernley towards the road (plate 26a) so as to obtain extra accommodation for a larger shop. Up to street numbering this extension was known as Gable End. He then proceeded to build up a very successful business (22) which flourished until about 1900 when he sold it to his shop manager, Mr Randell, who, after a short period of time, closed the business down, with the buildings being turned over to domestic accommodation. Gable End (plate 26a centre left) was eventually acquired by Neil Parsons whilst the rear section, Fernley (plate 26b), was occupied by Mr and Mrs Eaglen. On the departure of Mr and Mrs Eaglen from Fernley in the 1980s this rear property was also acquired by Neil Parsons and, after much renovation, has now been converted with Gable End into one single unit known as 76 The Street (plate 26c).

The old warehouse (plate 26a right) has, over the last few years, been very carefully renovated by the owner, Neil Buttifant, and was, up to the 1980s, the home of Mr Mortimer, a local artist, who left several examples of his work as murals on the wall of this old warehouse. After renovation Mr Buttifant let out the building to tenants but has now become the occupier after more recent renovation. The old bakery now known as Cluny 78 The

Plate 26a

Plate 26b   *Year 1951*

Plate 26c   *Year 1988*

Street was, after the Second World War, eventually bought by Miss Barrett and Miss Chipp, both of whom had retired from their nursing careers. In 1992 the dwelling was bought by Patrick Cox who then embarked on an internal renovation after which his mother, Mrs Nancy Cox, moved in. She shares the main entrance drive from the street with 76 The Street.

27
The National School
(Later The Church Room), The Street
T.575a

In 1836 a small piece of land at the rear of Ramplings (28), together with a narrow strip of land connecting this piece of land to the street, was conveyed from James Rampling to the Rev. R. E. Hankinson to enable him to build a school to accommodate forty children. It was opened in 1837 at a cost of £160 with Philip and Mary Armes being the first two teachers, followed by John Moss, Mrs Berry, Philip Frost, Harriett Wymer, James Arthurton, Edward Simcox and Rose Frost. Robert Hipper was the last teacher before the school closed after the 1870 Education Act was brought in and the Catholic School (83) was enlarged to accommodate all the village children.

The old National School, now owned by the Church Commissioners, remained closed until the Rev. J. J. Hampson renovated it and opened up a Sunday School here in 1906. During the First World War, 1914-1918, the building was used to accommodate civilian zeppelin spotters who had their observation post at the top of Costessey Tower (plate 124c). It remained as

Plate 27

51

a Church Room until well after the Second World War, being used by the Toch H, Parochial Church Council, Brownies and up to the end of the 1980s by the children's playgroup, until it was closed due to lack of maintenance. It was then, in 1993, bought by Lindsay Lock who owned the adjacent property, Roes Corner (29).

28
Ramplings, 86 The Street
T.278

In 1810 James Rampling bought this piece of land from Matthew Barker on which he built this cottage for himself and his wife, Elizabeth. In 1836 he sold off a piece of the land for the National School (27). He died in 1842 and his widow sold the cottage to Charles Hunt in1843. Charles Watcham acquired it in 1855 selling it to J.T. Boardman, a Norwich merchant, in 1881 who then sold it to William Champion. Mary Waters bought it in1887 and sold it in 1907 to Mary Wilkins. On her death, her younger brother, Charles, acquired it and lived here for many years until his death in 1943 at the age of 83. His widow, Charlotte, continued as owner occupier until her death in 1952 at 92 years of age. Her son succeeded but the cottage had deteriorated to such an extent that it was, in 1961, scheduled for demolition. It was, however, saved from this fate and a series of renovations were started. Mr and Mrs Patrick Cosgrave lived here until the early 1980s.

Plate 28

29 (L)
Roes Corner, 88 The Street
T.281

This property was owned by the Costessey Estate and is listed as such in the 1840 Tithe Award, but it goes back much further as Col. Glendenning identified an old Georgian fireplace which had been built into an old Tudor fireplace. The thick walls at the gable-ends are of brick and flint. The front and back walls were originally lath and plaster which points to an original timber-framed house built during the 1600s with additions in the 1700s and the 1800s when Georgian so-called improvements were carried out. It is thought to have been one of the very small farms that were in the street, as it had a barn structure to the east side of the building which was demolished after 1880 and two brick cottages built upon the old barn foundations (plate 56b).

The property was known as Roes Corner traditionally named after William Roes who, in 1892, was a tenant landlord at the nearby Black Swan (32) and later a tenant of a semi-detached cottage nearer to the corner (30).

At the 1918 Costessey Estate sale the whole property was withdrawn at £350, but, afterwards, the two brick cottages were bought by Mr S.Kirby (56). A Mr Foster bought Roes Corner and lived in one part with William Paul occupying another part. In 1961 Roes Corner was unoccupied and scheduled for demolition. It was, however, saved and listed by the Dept of the Environment as a building of Special Architectural and Historic Interest. The date was given in their report as early 17th century.

The property eventually became owned by Mr Rowe who lived at Merry Meeting (56). At his death, his wife, Vera, succeeded and in 1972 sold Roes Corner to Lindsay Lock, who has recently bought the adjacent Church Room (27).

Plate 29

30
94, 96 and 98 The Street
T. 235

Eldon Money came to Costessey about 1764 and is the first known owner of the land on which these three cottages now stand. They were eventually owned by Issac Cannell who, in 1855, sold out to the Costessey Estate. At this time there were five cottages on this site, two being quite small and at the rear of number 94 The Street, and the five tenants were William Rodgers, Harry Paul, William Dyson, Nicholas Baker, and Paul Austin. Although shown on the 1880 Ordnance Survey map, the two small cottages were demolished before the turn of the 20th century, probably by the Costessey Estate, still the owners at that time.

At the Costessey Estate sale in 1918 the three remaining cottages were occupied by William Roes (29) and Mr Forrest in the semi-detached cottages and John Wells in the larger detached cottage, now 94 The Street. John Wells was a painter and decorator, and he had, his paint shop, cart-shed and stable at the rear of his house, probably on the site of the two demolished cottages. He bought the house after the sale of the Estate, and lived here until his death. His son, Charles, sold the property and moved into the next door semi-detached cottage where he lived until his death in 1982 at 90 years of age. He went all through the First World War in trench fighting without even getting a scratch and, as he told the writer of this record, 'I never thought I would see Costessey again as my mates were falling down all around me'. In his later years his house became rather dirty and uncared for and he would not allow people into his home unless they had a permit ticket firmly affixed to a bottle of whisky.

After his death in 1982 the property was completely renovated by the owner, Edward Carver, and eventually sold to William McKenna in 1986. Mr Carver also owned the other cottage of the semi-detached pair of cottages, known as Ringrose Cottage 98 The Street which is now used as a weekend cottage. The name is derived from a past tenant, Mrs Ringrose, who lived here for many years until her death. 94 The Street was known as The Patch and, by will of a friend, left to John Folkard. He died in 1976 and the property was bought by Reginald Rees.

Plate 30 *Year 1951*

Photograph (30) shows 96 - 98 The Street on the right. Far left is St Mary's (33) with a Norwich Thorpe Station to Costessey Church number 3a bus photographed in 1951 travelling towards the church.

31 (L)
The Street Farm, 100 The Street
T. 560

As Eldon Money owned the land on which this property was built in 1775, it is more than probable that he it was who built it with the adjacent stable and barn. The farm included three acres of farmland between the house gardens and Folgate Lane on which Folgate Close was eventually built.

The first mention of this property in the Manorial Records was when Vernon Abbott sold it to Philip Copeman in 1812, who then sold it to John Sidney in 1826 for £1,150. The 1840 Tithe Award gives John Sidney as the owner with Jacob Cannell as the occupier. He apparently left in 1851 when John Sidney moved in himself and it remained in the Sidney family until 1874 when Stephen Hubbard bought it. It was let to William Thrower in the 1880s and, when he left, John Ireson became the occupier. When Stephen Hubbard died in 1900 the Costessey Estate acquired the property, known then as Street Farm.

At the 1918 Costessey Estate sale the farm was described as a 'Desirable Freehold Smallholding' but it was withdrawn at only £430. At this time James Melton was the tenant. Eventually Alan Leggett, a grocer and baker (24), bought the property, the three-acre field being farmed by Harry Phillippo (48). The farmhouse was let to Edwin Scott about 1920 and he remained here until 1953.

About 1961 Street Farm and the adjoining three-acre field was sold to Mrs Violet Howes of Folgate Lane, mainly to safeguard the field from housing development. In 1963, Mrs Howes sold the old farmhouse to Norfolk Hoteliers Estates at which time Gertrude Jones was a tenant occupier. The field, however, was kept by Mrs Howes and farmed by Harry Phillippo. Norfolk Hoteliers Estates sold the old farmhouse and associated buildings to Peter Mallender who then embarked on an extensive modernisation of the old Street Farm which then became known as Meadow View. In 1971 it was sold to Norman Brooks who remained here until November 1976 when he moved out and bought Riverside (25) selling Meadow View to Hendrik and Paula Wassenaar, who then carried out further renovations including those to the stables.

Plate 31a   *Year 1918*

Plate 31b   *Year 1993*

32 (L)
The Old Black Swan Public House
104 - 106 The Street
T.555

The first known owner of this property was John Howes who owned much property in Costessey in the 1600s. His son, William, and daughter, Rose, succeeded him and sold it to Thomas Randell in 1730. Eventually Charles Morse took over in1853 and George Morse followed in 1882. He was later to become a director of Steward and Patteson, Pockthorpe Brewery, Norwich. Charles Miller, seen with his wife and daughter at the rear of the Black Swan (plate 32b) with James Wymer, a Costessey Estate woodman, seated at a table, was the last tenant of the Black Swan after landlords Cannell, Sissen and Roes (29) had left. He stayed for only a short time before he was moved to the Bush Public House (16) which was also owned by Steward and Patteson, and the old Black Swan was closed as a public house. It was then let to William Thrower who occupied Street Farm (31) next door and one of the old farm barns still exists, gable-end to the street adjacent to the old Black Swan.

Alan Leggett who bought much property in Costessey also acquired the old Black Swan and converted it into a pair of semi-detached cottages, now known as Swan Cottage and Swan House. Swan House was then occupied by Mr Potter who left in 1958, the cottage standing empty for the next six months after which Mr Leggett sold it to Raymond Hammond. Swan Cottage was sold to Mr Trott, a Norwich builder, and, after some renovation, he sold it to John McCluskey. He then sold it to Brenda Winterbon.

The building, which is long but narrow, stands almost on to the street and at the front had a stepped entrance to the public house (plate 32a) leading straight from the road. As these steps became a traffic hazard they were taken down by Mr Leggett before he sold Swan Cottage to Mr Trott. The ever-increasing traffic became a danger to the building itself so kerb stones were laid along the front of the whole building. The four banding irons, two with heart-shaped ends in each long wall, are interesting features on the front elevation. They have been dated as being 16th century.

Plate 32a   *Year 1900*

Plate 32b   *Year 1900*

33 (L)
St Mary's, 93 The Street
T. 65

Fixed to the wall near the front entrance to this building is a plaque dated 1977 which states 'This house has seen 21 Reigns' (plate 33a). This includes the Cromwellian period of 1653 to 1660. In 1951, Col. Glendenning described this property as a Tudor house in which, on entering the front door, one could look right up to roof level, the upper floors only being inserted during the 17th century. He dated the moulding of the front and rear doorways as 1500. The beams are plain indicating a timber-framed house, with the brick gable-end and chimney to the street being added much later. Photograph (33b) shows the building as existing in 1887 with the tiled roof apparently converted from a hipped roof to a gable-ended roof.

Early owners of this property are unknown until John Culley (53) bought it in about 1816 and rented it out to R. Mackenzie-Bacon, the owner and editor of the 'Norwich Mercury'. He died in 1844 after living in this house for 28 years. The property was then unoccupied for some time but, by 1860, Henry Culley (50) and (53) became the occupier and the name was changed from The Residence to Wensum Cottage.

Henry Culley died in1887 leaving his son, Ernest, as the occupier of Wensum Cottage until it was sold at the 1902 sale of the Culley Estate (53). William Gunton, owner of Costessey Brickworks, became the next

Plate 33a

Plate 33b
Year 1887

Plate 33C
Year 1926

Plate 33d
Year 1988

Plate 33e   *Year 1915*

Plate 33f   *Year 1915*

64

Plate 33g   *Year 1915*

owner and he carried out very substantial repairs. The front wall was refaced with Costessey brickwork (plate 33c) and the windows were enlarged and replaced as were the roof and chimneys. William Gunton was on the Board of Guardians for the Wicklewood Poor Law Institution and he annually arranged for a group of residents to spend a day in his garden at Wensum Cottage (plate 33e) where croquet (plate 33f) and tennis (plate 33g) were also played.

William Gunton left Costessey in 1921 and Wensum Cottage was then sold to H. C. Greengrass (23) who, after more renovations, sold it in 1930 to John Hill, a school master, who remained living here until 1950 when the property was acquired by Dr Murphy and the house name changed to St Mary's. He then acquired extra land from Riverside (25) to provide a safer vehicle access. Dr Murphy left Costessey in 1969 after selling out to Charles Blundell OBE who, in 1981, sold the property to Bruce and Janice McKenna who have carried out further renovations on this very old Tudor property.

34

Cottages
95 - 97 The Street
T.67 and T.147

This row of four small cottages was built by John Culley on the site of four detached small cottages, two at the roadside and two at the rear which were demolished after he had obtained the Culley property at the 1879 sale. They had been occupied by Mrs Page, Robert Ottaway, Mrs Wymer and James Futter. The small cottages were designed for workers at his nearby Costessey Mill (53), and each had a rear exit on to a common passageway to the street. They remained in the Culley family until the final Culley sale of 1902 when they were bought by William Gunton. He sold up in 1921 to H. C. Greengrass, a Norwich builder who, in renovating, converted them into two larger cottages, each being given a front door entrance into the street.

In 1961 the owners were Mr Havran and Terence Youngman who sold out to Trevor Dann. Michael Hubbard acquired one of the cottages in 1981 and ten years later, when Mrs Smith had left her end cottage, this was also acquired by Michael Hubbard. He then converted the two cottages into one large cottage where, in 1902, there were four small cottages.

Plate 34

35
Malthouse Barn
99 The Street
T.63

The first known owner of this property was John Howes who was mentioned in the Manorial Records of 1670. The 1840 Tithe Award lists Hotson Cooper as the owner of the malthouse, but by 1843 the property had been sold to William Rogers. He died in 1854 and his widow sold out to James Linall, a wood carver employed at Costessey Hall. He died in 1887 and his daughter sold out to Charles Clark, a corn merchant from Norwich, in the early 1900s, but after his death the property gradually deteriorated. Malting had finished by this time and the building, hard against the street, had become a pair of semi-detached cottages with only one being occupied after the Second World War, by Elizabeth Wilkins. She sold out to Trevor Dann (34) who then set about restoring the old malthouse and, after obtaining an award for his design and workmanship from the Costessey Society, sold out to David Cheesman in 1981.

Plate 35

36
Greta Cottage and The Lime Kiln
111 The Street
T.161

As with the adjacent malthouse property, the first known owner is John Howes. Thomas Cooper acquired it about 1801 and retained it for thirty-three years, selling it in 1834 to Eldon Money (junior) who then let out part of the field to John Davey, a Norwich miller. This part then became known as Davey's Pyghtle (a small field). It is assumed that Eldon Money then started up the lime kiln here as Costessey lime was in great demand for the building of Costessey Hall (125). As the excavated chalk from this site contained more than the average proportion of flint stones, it is reasonable to assume that Greta Cottage, with its flint walls, was constructed from these flints as was Ivy Cottage (60) in The Croft. John Pilgrim is shown as the owner of Davey's Pyghtle and the lime kiln on the 1840 Tithe map, but this map does not show Greta Cottage. However, it is shown on the 1880 Ordnance Survey map, so it must have been built between these two dates.

Henry Steward was the owner in 1862 with Henry Banham obtaining it in 1874 for £150. This most probably was for Greta Cottage as the lime kiln was getting run down and finally finished about 1880. Henry Banham died in 1914 after which Greta Cottage was sold to Mrs Crossfield and her sister, Miss Chandler, who had moved down from Lancashire. Mrs Crossfield had a very extensive timber bungalow built adjacent to Greta Cottage. In this bungalow she kept herself, her pony and her dogs. She was a professional dog breeder and the first lady judge to officiate at Crufts dog show. About 1923 both Mrs Crossfield and Miss Chandler moved to Folgate Lane, then known as Sandy Lane, and here Mrs Crossfield built another timber bungalow for herself and her pony, and almost duplicating the premises just vacated. This bungalow still exists to the front of Crossfield Cottage, Folgate Lane.

Mr and Mrs George Powell then became the owners of Greta Cottage and Greta Bungalow. Mr Powell died in 1938 after which Mrs Powell married Mr Cushing and remained living in Greta Cottage. In 1959 Greta Bungalow

Plate 36

was let to Mr and Mrs Copland, but in 1971 they became the owners of both Greta Cottage and Greta Bungalow. In 1996 they started renovating Greta Cottage for their own occupation but, unfortunately, Mr Copland died early in 1997 shortly after moving in.

37

Hall View and River View
110 and 112 The Street
T.18

Hall View was so named because it was possible to see Taverham Hall across the valley before building development took place on the opposite side of the road. The first mention of this old house is when John Mountain sold it to Jeffrey Alcock in 1729, and in 1801 it was sold with the malthouse (35) to Thomas Cooper. Photograph (37a) shows the extensions carried out through the years to this old building. In 1837 Messrs Mann and Clarke , auctioneers, sold this property to James Banham for £241. He then sold part of the land to the north to his son, also named James, and he built himself a house in about 1845 which he named River View. James Banham (senior) died in 1854 and, after the death of his widow, Elizabeth, in 1860, Hall View was bought by Jacob Cannell, a Costessey butcher, who carried on a butcher's business here until his death in 1889. His son, William, bought it in 1905 after the death of Maria, widow of Jacob Cannell. William Cannell had a butcher's shop further down the street against the old Tudor Barn (11).

Jeremiah Futter, a groom gardener, lived at Hall View for many years, and after his death, his grandaughter, Ruth Owens and her husband, John, became the owners. Edward Dunt occupied part of the property in 1963, and, after the death of Ruth Owens in 1968, he became owner of Hall View, now 110 The Street. He is a smallholder and runs a small haulage and transport service. River View (plate 37b) now 112 The Street was eventually acquired by Alan Leggett (24) and was at first used as rented accommodation, but was then sold to Sidney Keable, who died in1989 leaving the property to his daughter, Wendy Valentine. She turned it into two flats for rented accommodation only, not being willing to sell the property at the present time. She also runs the Redwings Horse Sanctuary.

Plate 37a

Plate 37b

71

38 (L)
Trinity Cottage, 120 The Street
T. 2, T. 8 and T. 553

This cottage, originally thatched (plate 38a), was a semi-detached building in the early 15th century. The first known owners were Francis Lowe who died in1637, followed by William Baldwin who died in 1693, and then followed by Robert Lock. By this time an extension had been built on to the south end of the cottage making it into a three cell building housing three tenants, each having one room upstairs and one room downstairs. In 1711 Robert Lock succeeded his father and then sold it in about 1719 to James Minns. John Burroughes bought it in 1740 and two years later sold it to Jeremiah Burroughes. In 1754 Jonathan Poppey became the owner and in 1790, sold it to James Gartham, a Norwich auctioneer. He died in 1800 and left the property to his housekeeper, Miss Slapp. She is the recorded owner in the 1840 Tithe Award, with the three tenants being Mary Harden, John Ireson and James Hostler. The next known owner was Steven Hubbard who bought it in 1874 and it remained in the Hubbard family until about 1900 when it was sold to the Costessey Estate.

At the 1918 Costessey Estate sale the property was sold to R. H. Tebb for £160. At this time the only recorded occupier was George Ireson, paying a rent of just over £5 per annum. The sheds and stables he had built on the site were his own property and were not included in the sale. He was a waggoner at Costessey Mill and is seen on the extreme right (plate 53c). W. J. Pollard, manager of Costessey Mill, became the next owner until 1920 when the cottage was acquired by Mrs Grey, and she remained here until 1945 when John Wiltshire, a Norwich solicitor, bought it.

Adjacent to the north boundary was a row of three cottages. The 1840 Tithe Award lists Randell Adams as the owner and they remained in the Adams family until 1868 when William Champion bought them. He died in 1886 and they were then bought by Steven W. Fitt. Before the Second World War the three cottages were bought by Mr Blake and were occupied by Mrs Bumphrey, Mr Lowe and Mr Rice. As the cottages were becoming unfit for human habitation, the tenants were re-housed, and Mr John Wiltshire acquired the property. He demolished all but the roadside cottage in which a small letterbox can still be seen in the front door.

Trinity Cottage originally had a thatched roof (plate 38a) but this was destroyed in 1958 when a bonfire in an adjoining field (31) got out of hand and the wind carried sparks from the fire on to the thatch (plate 38b). A local architect, F. H. Swindells, drew up plans for restoring the cottage. He saved the external walls but replaced the thatch with a pantiled roof.

Plate 38a
Year 1951

Plate 38a
Year 1951

Plate 38c

Year 1988

39 (L)
Glen View and row of Three Cottages
113 -119 The Street
T.1 and T.5

The first mention of the old cottage that stood on the site of the present day Glen View was in 1657 when John Howes acquired it. It then passed through many recorded owners and in 1887 Stephen W. Fitt bought it, with the adjoining land and farm buildings, from William Champion, who had owned the property since 1868. Stephen Fitt had the old cottage pulled down and on the site he built a 17-room residence (plate 39a). In 1898 he vacated the residence and Dr J. J. Johnson moved in as tenant . He was the first medical man to live in Costessey, doing his visiting rounds in a pony and trap driven by his groom who occupied the central cottage of the now three cottages that adjoin Glen View (plate 39b).

The central cottage was, at one time, free standing and listed as being late 17th century. Wall panelling in one of the ground floor rooms is of the 18th century period and has 'raised and fielded panels, moulded cornice and dado rail and coved recess with ribs springing from a gilded pewter shell' (D. of E. 1983). One bedroom is partially panelled and has an 18th century door.

In the 18th century, lean-to buildings were added to either side of this 17th century central building and these would have been used for stabling and the storing of hay. These lean-to buildings were raised in the 19th century to match the height of the central building and were built with thicker 3 inch bricks than those of the central cottage. They were first mentioned at the Manorial Court in 1836 when Randall Adams acquired them from William Adams.

In the early 1920s Dr Johnson moved out of this rented accommodation into his new home in Longwater Lane, and Stephen Fitt returned to Glen View and remained here until his death in 1925. The property remained in the Fitt family until 1953 when it was sold to Mr Harden, and on his death in 1989, it became the property of Mrs Olive Harden. The adjacent cottage now belongs to Mr Roy Rowland. The remaining two cottages are also privately owned, the central cottage by Andrew Ulph and the end cottage by Jacqueline Cook.

Plate 39a

Plate 39b

40

Aerial Photograph

This aerial photograph, taken in 1951, is of the junction of Folgate Lane and The Street. Slightly above centre is an old thatched house T.587 belonging to the Trustees of the Great Hospital. Just the other side of the old thatched farmhouse, were two old cottages T 602a and these were occupied in 1840 by Joseph Girdlestone. The next occupier was Giles Read who was followed by his son, Ernest. These cottages then became very dilapidated and Ernest Read moved into the old thatched farmhouse with his family in about 1910. The old pair of semi-detached cottages were demolished after the First World War and Ernest Read used the cleared site as a garden. He died in the 1960s leaving his son, Charles, and daughter, Maggie, as tenants of the Great Hospital. The land was eventually sold as building land and has now been fully developed.

Behind the group of trees on the opposite side of the road is a piece of land listed in the Tithe Award T.603a and the Manorial Records as Rectory Land and also belonging to the Great Hospital. This land was worked by Charles Read as a market garden until it was also sold for building development, now 132 -134 The Street. He then moved from the old thatched farmhouse to a modern bungalow in Folgate Lane, where he remained until his death in1989.

Against the road but to the right of the old farmhouse and the adjacent farm buildings , can be seen the earthmark foundations of the large barn (41). At the top left hand corner is the thatched Trinity Cottage and in front of it is the row of three old cottages (38) and opposite, across the road, are the row of three cottages and Glen View (39). At the bottom corner on the right is a group of very old buildings (42). All the undeveloped land seen in this 1951 photograph has now been developed for building.

Plate 40   *Year 1951*

77

41

Fitt's Barn
T. 587

Towering above the word 'Cocoa' on the bus is the old farm barn referred to in (40). This barn belonged to the Great Hospital and was rented out to Stephen Fitt as a furniture store. He also rented it out for social or anniversary occasions (22). After the barn was demolished, the brickwork at the road edge was reduced in height and it housed a Post Office letter box. This was re-sited just into Folgate Lane in the 1960s when the roadside wall was demolished for building development. In front of the barn is the Costessey to Thorpe Station United Bus which started up a service in about 1925 and put all small transport village services out of business (82).

Plate 41   *Year 1930*

42 (L)
Old Tudor House, 138 The Street
T.60

The 1840 Tithe Award lists William Cater as the owner and John Downes, a carpenter, as the occupier. William Cater also owned the adjoining cottages (43). William Groves, a retired bricklayer from London, bought the property in about 1890 and was the owner and occupier up to 1914 when he hanged himself in one of his sheds. Mrs Lily Baker then bought the property and, when the United Bus Service started up in about 1925 with the terminus outside her house, she opened up the Rustic Tea Rooms in her garden. This attracted only a limited trade and after a few years she closed it up. Local history also mentions that a jam-making business was carried out here, and perhaps Mrs Baker was associated with this project. Also, at one period of its history, tradition mentions it as a public house because of a spacious wine and beer cellar, and later as a temporary furniture store in connection with Fitt's Barn (41). The next on record as owners

Plate 42a

Year 1951

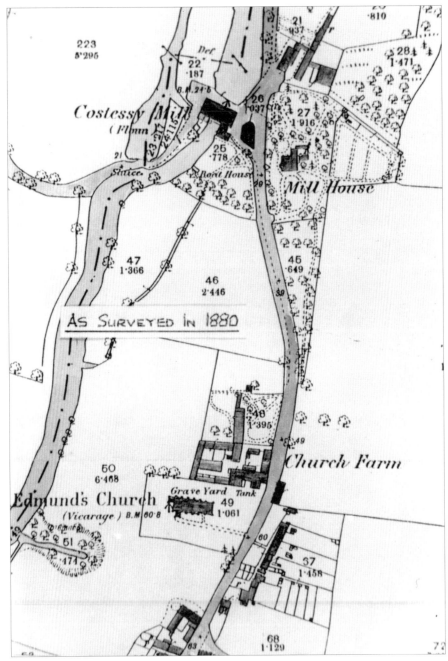

Costessy Mill
(Flonn)

Mill House

As Surveyed in 1880

Church Farm

Edmund's Church
(Vicarage)

Grave Yard

Plate 42b

Year 1880

80

Year 1993

were the two Flatman brothers who ran a smallholding up to 1950 when they both died.

The firm of Gibson Brothers bought it and, after renovations had been carried out, they sold the property to Clifford Godbalt. He remained here until about 1967 when John Insall, a local artist of some repute, bought it. He died in 1991 but his widow Anne, succeeded and remained as owner-occupier. In 1994 she married Dr Andriea L. Laubscher, and in 1997 sold the old Tudor House to Mark Kerrison.

The 1880 Ordnance Survey map (plate 42b) shows Fitt's Barn (41) at the bottom with another small building nearly opposite, and just above this is the old Tudor house (plate 42a) with the long range of buildings described in (43) and (44). Above these is the old farm cart-shed (46) and across the road is the Tithe Barn (47). Just above this is the old Church Farm and old Vicarage (48). Near the top of the map is Mill House now known as Costessey House (50), and then on to Costessey Mill (53) and Mill Cottages (51).

43 (L)
Two Old Tudor Cottages
140 - 142 The Street
T.57 and T.62

These two old cottages are also dated as 17th century and the 1840 Tithe Award lists William Cater as the owner. Between the two world wars the end cottage was occupied by William Baldwin, a male nurse at a mental hospital. After his death in 1964, his widow, Pamela, and her daughter, Angela Lince, remained as tenants of Mr Phillippo, a local farmer at Church farm, but he decided to upgrade the cottage by installing a bathroom and indoor toilet. He then raised the rent from 7 shillings per week to 35 shillings per week. Both Mrs Baldwin and Mrs Lince died in 1987. The cottage then became almost derelict, and, because of it being part of a listed building, administrators of the now late Mr Phillippo's estate were requested to make it safe. This was then carried out but a dispute arose over the land at the rear of the property. Although this has now been settled, the administrators seem to be reluctant to sell the property, which again shows signs of neglect.

Plate 43

The central small cottage was also owned by William Cater and was, at one time, occupied by Amy Young. For many years between the two world wars it remained unoccupied but, because of shortage of accommodation for evacuees during the Second World War, it was renovated up to a minimum standard for evacuees. After the Second World War, Edward and Molly Brett moved in but only stayed for a short period. It then became unoccupied but was eventually bought by John Insall, owner of the next door Tudor house (plate 42a) and was connected to his house to form one single dwelling as seen on the right (plate 43).

At the rear of these cottages was a group of very small cottages, the only access from the street being a footpath which crossed in front of Mr Phillippo's house (44) and then turned to follow a narrow footpath between the hedges. This is clearly shown on the 1951 aerial photograph (plate 45a) at the bottom right hand corner. These small cottages were also owned by Mr Cater and were occupied in 1840 by R. Anderson, a lime burner; William Adcock, William Doggett, a carpenter; Samuel Downes, a tailor; and, at the far end, Stephen Sisson. The cottages are shown on the 1840 Tithe map, but not on the 1880 Ordnance Survey map (42b), only the gardens which were the subject of the administrative difficulties mentioned earlier.

44

Cottages Opposite The Church
144 The Street

This row of three small cottages with a gable-end to the road and opposite the south burial ground of the church was not recorded in the Tithe Award of 1840, but they are shown on the 1880 Ordnance Survey map (plate 42b). They each had a small front garden but no land whatsoever at the rear. The gardens at the front extended as far as the right-of-way footpath to the five small cottages previously mentioned in (43). It is probable that this group of three cottages was built by William Cater who owned the land and all the other properties around this courtyard before selling the whole group of properties to William Groves in1890.

Mrs Lily Baker (42) became the next owner sometime after the First World War and later, after the Second World War, Harry Phillippo, a farmer at Church Farm, became the owner with the three tenants being Mr Briggs, Mr Horn and Mr Trett. When their tenancy ended in the early1960s the whole building was cleared and extensive renovations began. The three small cottages were converted into one larger property and an attractive extension to the central cottage was created. Remedial action was successfully taken when the street side gable-end developed an external bulge, but the effects can still be seen. On completion of the renovations, Mr and Mrs Wicks took up residence here after leaving Church Farm where they had been employed by Mr Phillippo as farm worker and housekeeper. When the house became unoccupied it was, once again, turned into a three cell building with Messrs Culling, Grint and Hipper being listed as tenants in 1995. However, in 1996 the three cottages had reverted to one single dwelling with Patrick Green as the occupier.

Plate 44

45
Aerial View, St Edmund's Church
The Street
T. 606a

This aerial view (plate 45a) taken in 1951 shows centrally, at the bottom edge, the old Tudor house (42a), the old houses adjoining it (43) and the three cottages with the gable-end to the road (44). Next to this property is a long row of seven cottages locally known as The Barracks. They were built in 1816 and each had only two rooms. The owner in 1840 was Anthony Bailey and they were occupied by Lucy Frost, Benjamin Fairman, Philip Gunton, Samuel Wymer, John Ireson and William Ireson, with the owner, Anthony Bailey, occupying the larger end cottage. One morning in June 1844, the wife of William Ireson lit the copper fire and then went to see a neighbour. On returning home she found that the fire had spilled out on to some dry sticks and filled the cottage with smoke suffocating their three little daughters, Emma, Maria and Elizabeth.

In 1890 the cottages were bought by William Groves who owned the adjacent property (44). After the First World War, Mrs Lily Baker became the owner but she sold most of them, retaining one for her own occupation. Before the Second World War the cottages were condemned and the tenants were re-housed in Folgate Lane (62), but before the cottages could be demolished the Second World War had started and they were used to house evacuees. They were finally demolished in the late 1950s with only the three cottages adjacent to Phillippo's cottage (44) being retained. These end cottages were later converted into two larger cottages, St Nicholas and St Edmundsbury, but these two have now been converted into one residence known as St Edmundsbury, owned by Brian and Lesley Smith. They speak of it being haunted by a 'happy ghost' who, when no person is present, moves household items around.

Further on past this row of cottages is the cart-shed, now demolished (plate 46). Across the road and opposite the old Tudor house (plate 42a) is the southern burial ground before the present church car park was prepared. Next to this is Costessey Church with its full complement of lime trees. In the early 1980s these trees were surveyed by tree inspectors and two trees were found to be dangerous, but when they were felled, at great expense to church funds, the trees were found to be perfectly sound and safe. About 1900 the lime trees had not even been planted (plate 45b) so they were of no great age in the early 1980s. Further along the road is the Tithe Barn (plate 47) and the Church Farmhouse with the adjoining Vicarage (48). Over to the left is the River Wensum flowing down towards Costessey Mill (53).

Plate 45a
Year 1951

Plate 45b
Year 1890

46 and 47 (L)
Old Cart-shed and Tithe Barn
The Street
T.91 and T.92

For many years this old cart-shed stood against the roadside opposite the Tithe Barn. In the 1840 Tithe Award, it was listed as Cart-shed and Plantation, and owned by John Culley who, at this time, was the owner of Church Farm. It was open to the roadway which allowed farm vehicles to be driven in straight from the roadway and for years it contained nothing but obsolete and rusting farming equipment, especially during the tenure of Harry Phillippo who apparently paid little attention to the derelict state of this structure and the dangerous condition of the sagging roof.

The problem was solved when Capt. Dawson of Costessey Park House (124) took over Church Farm and installed his son, John, as farm manager. During this time, the Tithe Barn roof was also getting into a very derelict condition (plate 47) and, being a listed building, John Dawson was required to repair the roof of this barn and to use matching tiles. These tiles were readily available from off the roof of the old cart-shed and were used to repair the barn roof. The cart-shed was then demolished.

The Tithe Barn has a date stone of 1688 on the gable-end facing the road, but very little is known of the history of this old barn. It is mainly a timber-framed building on dwarf brick walls. The gable-end to the street has return brick walls and is distinct from the timber framing. It has a very complicated roof structure to support the heavy pantiled roof. Over the years it has been used for occasional social purposes and added accommodation for Church Flower Festivals. Like the farmhouse, it is now owned by James Larke, a Norwich business man.

Plate 46   *Year 1984*

Plate 47   *Year 1984*

48
Church Farm and Old Vicarage
The Street
T.92

There is no doubt that the old building seen on the right (plate 48) is the old vicarage and it is described as such in the 1841 Census. Col. Glendenning in his notes on old houses in Costessey said that it was probably built at the same time as the Tithe Barn, 1688, perhaps using materials from a much earlier building on this site as the attic roof construction used methods in vogue before this time. The upper storey rooms also contained door panels of the William and Mary period, 1688-1702. The old vicarage was renovated in the 1740 period but by the early 1800s it was closed as a vicarage, the incumbents from then on having to find accommodation in private houses in the village until the building of the vicarage in Folgate Lane (63). By 1961 it was in a derelict condition and, although a listed building, it was completely demolished by the tenant of Church Farm, Harry Phillippo.

The building seen to the left of the old vicarage was built by John Culley about 1820.He was a leading Norfolk farmer and lived at Church Farm until his death in 1857.He was succeeded by his grandson, also named John, who farmed the land until his death in 1894.

The Culley Estate was sold up in 1902, and the next tenant in the farmhouse was Joseph Harris with John Blake as owner. Walter Coleman became the next tenant in 1923 and stayed until 1946 when Harry Phillippo became the tenant farmer and occupied the farmhouse with Mr and Mrs Wicks (44). When he died the Wickses moved out into the recently renovated cottage (44) opposite the church, and Capt. Dawson of Costessey Park House (124) bought the farm and installed his son, John, to manage it. He demolished the old farmhouse and built a modern farmhouse (plate 48b) on the site. However, the farm failed and the farmhouse, together with the Tithe Barn and the adjoining paddock, was sold to James Larke, a Norwich business man.

Plate 48a   *Year 1925*

Plate 48b   *Year 1993*

49

Approach To Costessey Mill

The photograph (49a) dated 1902 shows the roadway known as The Street leading down to the River Wensum and Costessey Mill. The first turning on the left would have led to the mill office, now a private residence known as Mill House (52) and a small loading bay of the mill reserved for local bakery customers. The small tree and shrub area with timber railings was removed about 1925 when the Norfolk County Council bought the private roadway running round the mill to upgrade the Drayton to Costessey lane.

The River Wensum is shown in the centre of the scene and to the right of it can be seen traces of the private roadway which led to Bridge Cottage (plate 55b) and the Toll Bridge over the River Wensum, and then on to the Drayton Low Road (plate 55c). The horse and waggon, together with the crossing cattle behind it, blocks the main view of this roadway. On the extreme right is the boundary wall of Costessey House (plate 50). This wall still exists. In 1901 a strong gale brought down this tree (plate 49b) across the road leading down to the River Wensum and Costessey Mill.

Plate 49a   Year 1902

Plate 49b   Year 1901

93

50
Mill House (now Costessey House)
The Street
T.101

After the death of John Culley in 1857, his son, Henry Utting Culley, took over the working of Costessey Mill (53) and then built this substantial residence in what was previously the garden of the original Mill House and office (52) across the road. He remained living here until his death in 1876, his widow staying on until her death in1887. Mill House was then taken over by her grandson, Albert Culley, whose father, Henry, and brother, Ernest, were living in Wensum Cottage (33). After the death of their father, Henry Culley, Albert and his brother, Ernest, jointly ran Costessey Mill but soon ran into debt losing much of the money their grandfather had made. Many financial disagreements occurred between the two brothers which ended when Ernest shot Albert whilst out on a shooting event over their land. It could never be proved whether it was by accident or design but many local people who knew of their financial difficulties, mainly caused by Albert, thought that it was no accident.

After Albert's untimely death in 1893, Mill House was let to Mr E. Rice who then lived here until the sale of the Culley Estate in 1902, when it was sold to Charles H. Finch,a director of Steward and Patteson, the owners of the Bush public house in The Street. He made many alterations and extensions to the south aspect of Mill House including a large billiard room and other extra accommodation. He lived here until his death in 1954 at 88 years of age by which time the house had been renamed as Costessey House. His widow remained living in Costessey House until her death in 1964 at the age of 92 after which the property was sold to Kevin Shortis, a Norwich motor accessory retailer, who has made more modern improvements to the house by adding extensions to the front of the building.

Plate 50   *Year 1902*

51
Mill Cottages
T.98

The 1840 Tithe Award describes this property as a house and garden occupied by John Culley, the owner of Costessey Mill (plate 53b), but at the 1879 Culley Estate sale there were two houses on this site with tenants Mrs Harvey and Mr Sissens, both of whom were given notice to quit, After the sale, the cottages were back in the ownership of the Culley family. At the rear of the cottages was a group of farm buildings, and an early tenant, Mr Springhall, is recorded as keeping cows there and selling milk.

At the final sale of the Culley Estate in 1902 the cottages, together with the Mill House, now known as Costessey House, were bought by Charles H. Finch who used these cottages as accommodation for his gardener, Mr Bell, and his chauffeur, Mr Houchen, who remained with Mrs Finch until her death in 1964. These two cottages were then acquired by Mr Kevin Shortis who had them cleaned and decorated, one being let to various tenants and the other as accommodation for a longstanding employee, Desmond Pye.

Plate 51

52
Mill House and Office
T. 95

In 1858 the old wooden mills (plate 53b) were demolished and a five-storey building erected in white brickwork (plate 53c). Adjacent to this new mill but built in red brickwork, was the Mill House and Office (plate 52a) in which all administration of the new mill was carried out. At the1924 fire when the new mill was burnt to the ground (plate 53d), this office accommodation was saved and was eventually bought by Charles Finch who, in 1902, had bought Mill House and renamed it Costessey House (50). He had this old Mill House and office enlarged and converted it into a private residence, Mill House, which was then let to Mr G. B. Johnson who moved out after the death of Mrs Finch, after which the property was sold.

There have been many owner-occupiers since 1965 and many of them have only stayed here for short periods, either because of the noise from flowing water or from the noise from visitors to the millrace area during the summer period (plate 52b). Five owners moved in and out between 1971 and 1981, after which it was sold to the present owner, Mr Jeremy Hulbert.

Plate 52a

97

Plate 52b   *Year 1951*

53
Costessey Mill
T. 95

Mills are mentioned as being on this site way back in the Domesday Book of 1087. The first known owner is John Hyrne who died in 1687. In 1745 the mill was derelict and was bought by William Pepper of Buxton who then built a new mill which was opened in 1751 (plate 53a). William Wilkin bought it in 1786. He died in 1799 and his son, Simon, succeeded but was a failure and eventually became bankrupt. A successful farmer from Ringland, near Costessey, John Culley, bought the mill in 1825 and installed his son, Henry Utting Culley, as the mill manager. He was so successful that after he succeeded his father in 1857, he had the old mill (plate 53b) taken down and, in 1858, had a five-storey mill built (plate 53c). Henry Utting Culley died in 1876 and his son, Henry, took over the running of the new mill whilst still living with his two sons, Albert and Ernest, at Wensum Cottage (33).

Plate 53a

Year 1800

99

The executors of Henry Utting Culley's Estate realised that the expensive building of the new mill 1858 had incurred vast amounts of money resulting in massive debts and they were compelled to put the whole Estate up for sale. This was organised by Messrs Spelman in July 1879 at the Norfolk Hotel, Norwich but, fortunately for the Culleys, a benefactor came forward and cleared all their debts and allowed them to continue milling operations at Costessey Mill. Henry Culley died in 1887 leaving his two sons to run the mill.

After the untimely death of Albert Culley in 1893 (50), Ernest Culley carried on the mill with W. J. Pollard as business manager but in 1902 the mill and estate had to be sold. G. W. Thompson, a miller from Marlingford, bought the mill and joined up with Mr W. Pollard, the previous manager, under the name of Thompson and Pollard until 1920 when it was sold to Price Brothers, who were millers with mills at various large ports. New machinery was installed, the noise from which, it was said, could be heard all over the village but not for long as the mill caught fire at 9 a.m. on the 8th July 1924 (plate 53d), apparently from a fault in an oil engine, and by 10 a.m. the fire was at its height making it impossible to cross the two

Plate 53b   *Year 1850*

Plate 53c   *Year 1900*

Plate 53d   *Year 1924*

bridges against the mill. Flames were soon roaring from all windows and only the ground floor was not then alight, which enabled Police Constable Porter, having heard a cat in distress, to crawl in at great risk to himself and rescue a black and white cat. Shortly afterwards all the upper floors and the machinery crashed down and, although there was a likelihood that the external walls would collapse, the firemen carried on and by 12.30 p.m. the fire was under control. For safety the external walls were later demolished and new walls built at roadside locations.

Mr Charles Finch who, in 1902, had bought the old Mill House now known as Costessey House (50), then bought the site of the burnt-out mill which also included the short section of roadway between the two bridges which he then sold to the Norfolk County Council to improve the road between Costessey and Drayton.

54
Bessy's Bridge
Costessey Lane Drayton

Although actually in Drayton, this old bridge has been included in this record because of its nearness to Costessey. Map (plate 55d) shows a ford and a footbridge where the lane from Costessey to Drayton crosses a field drainage channel. Many older residents of Costessey have known this humped-back bridge as 'Bessy's Bridge' and have said how difficult it was to walk over it pushing a pram. After the fire at Costessey Mill in 1924 (plate 53d) the private road against the mill was sold and the road to Drayton made up and presumably, at that time, this old bridge was demolished.

Plate 54a

Year 1912

Plate 54b   *Year 1920*

Plate 54c   *Year 1920*

55
Bridge Cottage and Toll Bridge
T.144

This Cottage with the Toll Bridge is shown on a Costessey Mill Estate sale plan of 1817 when the mill was owned by Wilkin and Durrant. In 1825 John Culley bought the mill together with the Bridge Cottage and the private roadway (plate 55a) to the bridge and over to the Fakenham Turnpike, now known as Drayton Low Road. Photograph (55c) taken in 1902 shows this junction with the Drayton Low Road. The small foreground bridge crosses a narrow field drain whereas further on can be seen part of the main bridge spanning the River Wensum. Map (55d) shows the route from Costessey Mill to both Bessy's Bridge on the left and Bridge Cottage at the top.

The 1841 Census lists William Downing and his wife Lucy, as occupants, with John Culley as the owner. After the death of William and Lucy Downing, the cottage was taken over by their daughter, Ann, who then had the responsibility of collecting bridge tolls from those wishing to cross the bridge (plate 55b). Bridge Cottage was re-thatched just before the turn of the century and, with the private roadway back to the mill, was included in the 1902 sale of the Costessey Mill Estate. Since being sold at that sale, Bridge Cottage, together with the private roadway, has had many owners. In the 1950s it had become derelict but was renovated and occupied by Catherine Brett who died in 1961. By then the thatched roof had been replaced by a tiled roof.

Plate 55a

Plate 55b   *Year 1887*

Plate 55c   *Year 1902*

The last owner of Bridge Cottage was Mr Moreton, a retired speedway rider who, it was said, had so many accidents that it affected his head, making him a person who preferred to live on his own, resenting any persons using his long private roadway to his cottage and the old toll bridge which, in the 1950s, was a safe footway. However, the Drayton Parish Council averred that it was a public right of way. This was disputed by the Costessey Parish Council who argued that the bridge was restricted to the owner of Bridge Cottage and the adjoining land. This was upheld by Mr Moreton who had refused to allow public use of the bridge. The discussions became inconclusive when the bridge became dangerous and was demolished. An iron girder was left in place across the river at this point to safeguard permission for any future bridge at this crossing. Mr Moreton then gave permission for, as he told the writer of this record, 'any fool wanting to cross the river'. After the 1994 floods Bridge Cottage became unfit for habitation and was demolished after Mr Moreton had moved away.

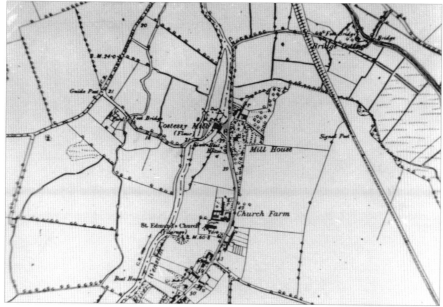

Plate 55d

Year 1905

56
Merry Meeting and Barn Cottage
The Croft
T. 245

These two cottages (plate 56b) were built after the 1840 Tithe Award on
the foundations of an old barn which is still shown on the 1880 Ordnance
Survey map (plate 56a). However, this barn was demolished by the
Costessey Estate who then built the two cottages. The frontage of these
cottages faces inward from the road and over the old farmyard area, whereas
the rear of the cottages is hard up against the road edge, with the ground
floor level being much lower than the road level making direct access from
the road very difficult.

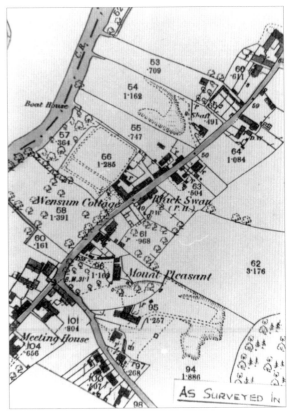

Plate 56a
Year 1880

Plate 56b

At the 1918 sale of the Costessey Estate, the tenants were S. Kirby, who had been a tenant for many years, with G. Minns occupying the adjoining cottage. Mr and Mrs Rowe were the owner-occupiers of Merry Meeting in the early 1960s until the death of Mr Rowe in 1972. About 1980 Alan and Margaret Saunders became the owners of Merry Meeting and in 1986 Ross and Nicole Willis acquired the next-door cottage now known as Barn Cottage. The 1880 Ordnance Survey map (plate 56a) shows the old barns adjacent to Roes Corner (29) and Mount Pleasant (57) now known as West Hill. Below this are the Lime Kiln (58), The Cottage in the Croft (59) and Ivy Cottage (60). Bottom centre are numbers 1 to 6 The Croft.

57

Mount Pleasant (now West Hill)
The Croft
T.559

Mount Pleasant was built by Eldon Money (senior) in about 1775 and he was the first owner-occupier. He also started off the adjacent lime kiln (58). Joseph Stannard bought Mount Pleasant in 1820, passing it to his daughter, Elizabeth Bond, in 1846 then to James Horne in 1856 and James Mayes in 1858. In 1864 James Mayes was living here to be followed by David Blunderfield, a farmer from Poringland, who bought it in 1873 and sold it in 1887 to Edward Spaul.

The Rev. George Badeley lodged here from 1896 to 1900 followed, it appears, by the Rev. John Hampson (63), with James Syder as tenant. He was a horse-dealer and eventually bought Mount Pleasant with borrowed money. When he died in1936 he left many debts and no assets.

Martin Kinder, an insurance agent from Norwich, eventually became the owner and he greatly modernised the property, making a south facing room

Plate 57

from which one of the finest views over Costessey can be seen. According to Kelly's Directory, he also changed the name to West Hill. After his death in the 1980s, his widow sold out to John and Angela Hollies who started up a business as Costessey Potteries. This closed down and the property was sold to Peter Nelson, an electronics engineer who carried on his business from here. This failed in 1996 and the property was then re-possessed and bought by Paul Birchall who then moved in after he had sold Knott Cottage (90).

58 and 59
Lime Kiln and Cottage in the Croft
T.229, T.230 and T.231

The first mention of the lime kiln in The Croft was in the Manorial Records of 1808 when Eldon Money's widow died and their son, Eldon, succeeded to the Money Estate. It is without doubt that Eldon Money (senior) built the kiln and started lime burning with his son, Eldon. By 1840 Eldon (junior) had sold out to John Pilgrim (36) but he continued to work the kiln as a tenant. After Eldon's death, John Pilgrim sold the business to James Cuddon who, in 1863, sold out to James Banham for £120. The kiln remained in the Banham family, but in about 1905 Charles Banham gave up lime burning and the kiln was never used again. Charles died in 1909 and his son, George, became the owner.

It was then that the Rev. John Hampson, vicar of Costessey, obtained permission from George Banham to start up a rifle club in the old chalk excavations which were adjacent to the Mount Pleasant property (57) and the Costessey Rifle Club was formed (plate 58b), with Stafford Henry Jerningham of Costessey Hall being a founder member. He eventually became Sir Henry Jerningham of Costessey Hall. Although the kiln has not been fired since 1905, it still exists in a sound condition today (plate 58a). The Cottage in The Croft (plate 59), which in 1840 was owned by

Plate 58a
Year 1984

112

Plate 58b
Year 1909

Plate 59

John Pilgrim, was occupied by John Norman as tenant and, like the kiln, was sold to James Banham in 1863.

Norman Hart, an insurance clerk, became the owner of The Cottage in the Croft and the lime kiln after the Second World War and, late in 1980, he attempted to obtain planning permission to develop a small area in the grounds of the now disused lime kiln. This was refused and the whole of the lime workings was then scheduled as a conservation area. Mr Hart eventually sold out to John and Susan Fisk in about 1993.

60
Ivy Cottage, The Croft
T.220

The 1840 Tithe Award lists Samuel Lovett as the owner-occupier of Ivy Cottage (plate 60a) centre background with (59) on extreme left. As this property was freehold, there are no other records but it is possible that it was built between 1800 and 1840, perhaps by John Pilgrim, as it is of similar construction to Greta Cottage (36) in The Street. Both are situated near a lime kiln which produced ample flints for their construction. Both lime kilns belonged to John Pilgrim before 1840. Before 1900 Edward Palmer, a miller employed at Costessey Mill, became the owner with his son, John, succeeding him in about 1905. The small garden of this cottage abutted on to arable land owned by the Costessey Estate and John Palmer obtained the adjacent plot of land that had previously been bought from the Costessey Estate for a Methodist chapel and then not required.

John Palmer remained at Ivy Cottage for many years and was eventually succeeded by his son, Frank. The next known owner was C. F. Farley who obtained it from Frank Palmer's widow in 1961. He remained here until about 1975 when Philip Sellars became the owner-occupier, since when the cottage (plate 60b) has been sympathetically extended to match the facing flintwork of the old building. A number of old bottles were found embedded in the old lime mortar walls.

Plate 60a   *Year 1900*

Plate 60b

115

61
1 - 4 The Croft
T. 222 and T. 223

These two pairs of cottages were, in 1840, owned by Henry Lovett who was a builder and he most probably built them in about 1830, using one cottage for his own use. He had his business located at Poplar Farm which he rented from Thomas F. Berney (108).

Plate 61

5 - 6 The Croft
T.182 and T.183

This pair of cottages was built at the same period as numbers 1 to 4 and was also built by Henry Lovett. The 1840 Tithe Award lists Mrs Hardy as the owner and at this period there were three cottages in this group, the tenants being William Skipper, James Futter and John Doggett. These cottages are also shown as a group of three on the 1918 Ordnance Survey map. However, the very small end cottage was taken into the adjacent cottage which makes number 5 slightly larger than number 6. Although these modernised cottages are now over 160 years old and adjoining a conservation area, they were not considered of sufficient historic interest to be included within the area, the boundary of which runs along The Croft between these cottages and Ivy Cottage opposite (60).

62
Folgate Lane

The 1840 Tithe Award lists the Trustees of the Great Hospital and the Costessey Estate as the main owners of land in Folgate Lane. Only the names of two local owners, John Sidney and George Carr, are retained in Sidney Road and Carr's Hill Close. In 1918 the Costessey Estate was sold off and, soon afterwards, the Great Hospital sold much land to the Forehoe and Henstead Rural District Council. Three groups of four small bungalows were then built for elderly people. They all had long gardens which were beyond the gardening capability of many of the aged residents. In the 1960s more land was acquired by the South Norfolk District Council and additional housing for the elderly was built. The long gardens of the original bungalows were used for infilling with further bungalows. On the adjoining site a group of ten steel-framed houses were built, but many of these have now been sold privately.

The land opposite this development was sold to Alan Leggett who had bought much land in Costessey. He built himself a bungalow and this can be seen on the far left of (plate 62a) which shows Folgate Lane in 1958. The remaining fields he let out to Harry Phillippo, a local farmer (48). It was from these fields that the fire was started that spread to the thatched roof of Trinity Cottage (plate 38b). The field in the near foreground was later sold to Violet Howes who, in about 1970, sold out to C. Trott, a Norwich builder, and Folgate Close was developed.

To prevent further building in this part of Folgate Lane, the wooded area known as Money's Hills was made the subject of a Tree Preservation Order which guarantees the retention of the rural atmosphere on this section of the lane. An interesting small gateway leads, for no apparent reason, into the wooded area just to the left of the farm gateway seen on the near left-hand bottom corner of (plate 62a). The 1938 Ordnance Survey map names this part of the lane as Folgate but from The Croft to Townhouse Road as Sandy Lane. The full length of the lane is now known as Folgate Lane.

The small gateway, mentioned above, was in a derelict state before the Second World War and could well have been referred to as a 'Folly' it leading, for no reason, into an undeveloped wooded area. Mrs Violet Howes had it re-built in about 1960 when she moved from Chescombe Lodge, Folgate Lane, and built a new house for herself next door, now known as Beacon House. It has again been re-built by the new owners of Beacon House who acquired the property in1990. It is possible that the present day name for this lane stems, in one way or another, from this very old gateway which will be referred to again in the building of the new vicarage (63). Photograph (plate 62a) was taken in 1958 from a point very near this old gateway, whilst (plate 62b) was taken from the same spot in 1993.

Plate 62a   *Year 1958*

Plate 62b   *Year 1993*

63
The Vicarage
Folgate Lane
T.593

The first mention of a vicarage or rectory in Costessey was on the 19th November 1732 when Thomas Martin, an historian from Thetford, visited Costessey and reported that the rectory (48) lay to the north-east of the church. The Rev. Thomas Watson was appointed to Costessey in 1821 and, finding no vicarage, took over the then vacant Woodside Cottage (68). He was followed by the Rev. James Evans who also used Woodside Cottage as a vicarage. He was followed by the Rev. George Badeley in1896, by which time Woodside Cottage was not available. The Rev. Badeley took up lodgings at Mount Pleasant (57) and remained there until 1900 when the Rev. John Hampson was appointed as vicar of Costessey.

According to Henry Gunton in his 'Gunton Papers', 1966, the Rev. Hampson then took up lodgings at a farmhouse in Drayton and rowed across the river whenever he wanted to come to Costessey. T.B. Norgate, in his 'History of Costessey', 1972, has copied the story from the 'Gunton Papers' but has moved the farmhouse to Hellesdon. Neither author mentions the farm by name nor the route taken to the church. Mrs Pamela Baldwin was born in 1893 and lived in the small Tudor cottage (43) opposite the church. She

Plate 63a   *Year c. 1914*

was an enthusiastic worker for the church, custodian of a church key and well versed in church history. She retained her fantastic memory up to her death in1987 at the age of 94. In a tape-recorded interview with Robert Atkins of Vicarage Close Costessey, in 1986, Mrs Baldwin clearly stated that the Rev. Hampson lodged at Mount Pleasant.

The Rev. Hampson quickly set about raising funds and, with help from the Queen Anne Bounty Fund, was able to commence building his new vicarage in Folgate Lane in 1901. If lodging at Mount Pleasant, now known as West Hill, he would be able to keep a close watch on the building of his vicarage by leaving at the rear of Mount Pleasant, passing the adjacent disused lime workings and, after a very short cut through Money's Hills, enter Folgate Lane via a gateway (62) opposite the vicarage building site. On this route he would also become aware of the very secluded lime workings in which he started up the Costessey Rifle Club (58). A gateway for a similar short cut to Folgate Lane is mentioned in section (68). The vicarage was completed in 1902, but being built on high ground the supply of water was a problem and required a deep driven pipe to be sunk and topped by a suitable pump, the remains of which still exist near the boundary of Vicarage Close.

During the interregnum between the Rev. Sedgley and the Rev. Bourne, the vicarage was used by Anglia Television for a production of 'Tales of the Unexpected'. The church was also to be used but as certain scenes did not meet with ecclesiastical approval, the already given permission was withdrawn. After the departure of the Rev. Collison in 1995, the vicarage was internally renovated prior to the arrival in 1996 of the Rev. Nicholas Parry.

Plate 63b   *Year 1995*

64

Windmill Cottage and Eastwood Mill
T. 276
Windmill Cottage (now Wensum View)
T. 277

Eastwood Mill was a post mill with a wooden base roundhouse and was built on the foundations of an earlier mill which belonged to Robert Fox and is still shown as such on a sale map of 1817. On the 6th October 1810, Edmund Martin inserted an advertisement in the 'Norfolk Chronicle' for a miller to work this windmill. The Manorial Records of September 1818 state that Edmund Martin, who had bought the windmill site off Robert Fox, had lately built the windmill.

Plate 64a   *Year 1902*

Robert Leeder became the miller for Edmund Martin and lived in Windmill Cottage to the west of the windmill whilst Edmund Martin, who was a farmer, built himself a cottage to the east of the windmill. This was also named Windmill Cottage. The 1840 Tithe Award lists R. Leeder and E. Martin as the occupiers of the two cottages. Edmund Martin advertised the windmill for sale in 1846 and again in 1852, but finally on the 27th November 1852, in the 'Norfolk Chronicle', it was offered for sale by Private Contract with the stipulation that the mill could be removed at any time before the 6th January 1853. It was neither sold nor removed and was, in

March 1858, still in the ownership of Edmund Martin but occupied by John Gotts. It was put up for sale again in 1858 with James Rumball as the listed miller. Spelmans, Auctioneers of Norwich, advertised it in 1861 and sold it to F. Banham and in 1863 it was in the occupation of John Rump, with John Gotts now working at the new water mill.

In the 'Norfolk News' dated 20th May 1865, an advertisement appeared which stated that Messrs Butcher would sell by auction the windmill and dwelling house occupied by John Rump at the low rent of £16 per annum. At this auction John Gotts became the owner but he later sold out to the Costessey Estate in1867 but remained at the windmill as tenant miller. John Rump had moved to the watermill and from 1868 to 1888 the windmill was in the occupation of John Gotts and Richard Gotts. It was finally advertised to be let in October 1889 but was not taken on. John Gotts transferred his milling experience to the modern watermill whilst John Rump returned to the windmill but failed to make it pay and the mill was shut down and never worked again.

A painting (plate 64b) by the writer of this record using old maps and drawings and with the help of a previous occupier, Miss Bumphrey, shows

Plate 64b

the windmill and sheds as they were in 1890. The gateway, at bottom centre, led to a well in the garden of Edmund Martin's house, which provided water for all residents living near the windmill. Henry Bumphrey became the next tenant and in 1893 the roundhouse base of the old windmill was used for the wedding reception for his son, George, when he married Priscilla Harvey. The rotating top section of the mill, the buck, which carried the sails and the machinery became in a very dangerous condition (plate 64a) and in 1902 was demolished. The roundhouse remained with the Bumphreys using it as a chicken shed.

At the Costessey Estate sale in 1918 Windmill Cottage was bought by the tenant, Henry Bumphrey, for £120 and it remained in his family until about 1958 when Graham Hunter, a curator of the Bridewell Museum, became the owner. He has been credited with the demolition of the old base roundhouse. Brian Knights, a quantity surveying engineer, then became the owner and remained here until about 1980 when he sold out to Mr and Mrs Gaunt. Windmill Cottage has now been renovated by Mrs J. Gaunt and in 1997 she sold it to Ian Richardson.

Also at the Costessey Estate sale, Edmund Martin's Windmill Cottage, which had been let to H. Ireson at a rental of £7 per annum, was bought

Plate 64c

by Mr Kirby for £130 and then sold to Mr Coleman for £145. In 1960 Mr and Mrs Nunn were the owners, Mrs Nunn being a member of the Costessey Drama Group. The cottage by this time had been renamed as Wensum View, and in 1971 became the property of Dr Glynn D. Brisley (plate 64c) and he has carried out several extensions and renovations.

65

Greenacres and Mockbeggars Townhouse Road

T. 513

Up to the death of the last Lord Stafford of Costessey Hall in 1913, it was the general policy of the Estate to buy up any land or property that came on to the market, even if this would mean the Estate having to raise the funds for conveyance by the security of a mortgage loan. It is therefore a reversal of this policy when, in 1906, Lord Stafford authorised the sale of two acres of The Plantation which bordered Townhouse Road and Folgate Lane to a local builder, Albert Palmer (102).

On these two acres Albert Palmer built two substantial better-class semi-detached houses costing £400 each. Put up for sale they found no buyer and Mr Palmer was obliged to offer them to let, the first tenants being his uncle, Frederick Gunton, and next door, Edmund Howard. The houses were named as The Plantation, on the left and Oakdene, on the right.

Records dated 1961 show Mr Clifford King as being the owner of The Plantation, now known as Greenacres, with George Patten as a tenant. In 1964 Greenacres was sold to the Church Missionary Society and occupied by the Rev. George Nicholson. He was followed later by the Rev. Ernest Wilks who remained here to about 1982 when the house was sold to Mr A. Davis. It was sold to Mr G. Boys in 1996.

In 1934 Oakdene, next door, was sold to W.G. Double and the house was renamed as Mockbeggars, quite an apt name after the sale of the site by Lord Stafford as, after entertaining Royalty, the landed gentry were often faced with vast debts to be settled when they would be obliged to sell off some saleable property and would then be known as Mockbeggars. Mr Double remained at Mockbeggars until about 1963 when he sold it to R. Dubbins who stayed here until 1967 when the property was sold to John and Sylvia Yates. They remained here for nearly thirty years eventually selling Mockbeggars to Dr Robert Koebner.

Plate 65   *Year 1918*

66
Woodlands
Townhouse Road
T.552

Sir William Jerningham of Costessey Hall,1774 to 1809, was responsible for the construction of a number of buildings in the village mainly for his family and senior members of the external staff, such as this head gamekeeper's cottage, now known as Woodlands. The 1840 Tithe Award lists Richard White as the gamekeeper occupying the cottage. He later left to take on West End Farm (104) and was followed by a Mr Morris who left about 1890 when James Archer moved in and stayed here until his death in 1905. William Stannard followed and was the last gamekeeper to occupy the cottage up to the sale of the Costessey Estate in 1918, when the cottage was withdrawn but was later bought by A. E. Priest who had previously bought Woodside Cottage now known as Eastwood Lodge (68).

The next owner was Col. H. Chapman, a District Councillor and also a Director of Mann Egerton. He modernised the interior and, in 1959, went in for intensive poultry farming, establishing large huts containing batteries well into the surrounding woodland. Unfortunately, in 1960, his stock of poultry was attacked by fowl pest and all stock had to be destroyed. After the required amount of time new battery hens were again producing eggs, some of which were on sale from a hut just inside the gateway. A few hens escaped from these batteries and had a happier life scratching a living in nearby gardens.

Col. Chapman eventually gave up battery hens and chicken farming and built a house on an adjoining plot of land, naming the property Pound House, and Woodlands was sold. It was eventually acquired by Mr and Mrs Sutton who sold out in 1991 to Mr and Mrs Stephen Smith.

Plate 66

67
The Coach House
Townhouse Road
T.551

At a convenient distance from Woodside Cottage, now Eastwood Lodge (68), Sir William built this brick and tiled coach house and stabling. At the 1918 sale of the Costessey Estate this property was sold integral with Woodside Cottage to Mr H. J. Bunbury, who, by the early 1920s, had sold out to Mr A. E. Priest, a Norwich motor- cycle engineer. He remained the owner up to about the late 1930s, after which he sold out to Mr E. E. Hines, also a Norwich engineer. After the death of Mr Hines in 1975, the Coach House was taken over by his elder daughter, Judith, who has turned the old coach house into a well-equipped art gallery. The Coach House and Gallery was put up for sale during 1997 and has now been acquired by Tops Property Services of Norwich.

Plate 67

68
Woodside Cottage (now Eastwood Lodge) Townhouse Road
T.550

This double-fronted cottage listed in the sale catalogue of the Costessey Estate as a 'Unique Freehold Bijou Residence' was built by Sir William Jerningham for his second son, The Hon. William Charles Jerningham, and here his five children were born. Parson Woodforde from Weston Longville, on visiting the cottage in 1796, described it as a new cottage and fitted out in a very tasty and fashionable manner.

In 1802 two friends travelled from Norwich in a gig drawn by a horse named Sharper and visited Sir William's cottage. The chronicler of the trip proceeds, 'This cottage is the centre one of three, built on nearly the same construction, the Gothic style, white washed, and thatched. The two outward ones are let, the other is entirely devoted to the pleasure of

Plate 68a   *Year 1909*

131

Plate 68b

Sir William, who frequently spends his afternoon here. This cottage is fitted up in the very first style of elegance. There are many valuable paintings and engravings, with some original and whimsical drawings. This cottage much resembles a palace in miniature, and like a palace, has its state bedroom and other appendages. An old woman resides in it, on purpose to keep the rooms and furniture in order, and to show the cottage to strangers'.

It appears that the Hon. William Charles and family were not in residence during this visit described in 'A Norfolk Excursion' and published in 'The Miniature Magazine' 1802, but in July 1809, Lady Jerningham of Costessey Hall paid a visit to the cottage and wrote later in her letters, 'George, Mrs Jerningham and I walked in the evening to William's cottage. Everything in this pretty dwelling is pleasant and comfortable, the sweet temper of its mistress would render any place so'.

The Hon. William Charles died in 1820 after which the cottage became vacant and then, in 1821, it was taken over as a vicarage by the Rev. Thomas Watson. He was followed in 1845 by the Rev. James Evans who stayed here until 1896, when, as an ill man, he made his long way back to Cardiff, only to die on the night of his arrival.

The cottage was then taken over by Mr and Mrs Oldfield as tenants of the Costessey Estate, but they left after obtaining the first known divorce in Costessey about 1909. They were followed by Mr William Price who is recorded as having presented St Edmund's Church, Costessey, with its organ, still in use today. He remained in the cottage until the 1918 sale of the Costessey Estate when the property was bought by H. T. Bunbury. He replaced the thatched roof with small roof tiles, the cottage then losing much of its picturesque appearance (plate 68a).

The next owner and occupier was Mr A. E. Priest, a Norwich motor and motorcycle engineer, who made more so-called improvements, detracting still further from this charming old residence. He did, however, reposition the entrance drive and planted a number of shrubs and ornamental trees in a garden which, in 1841 was described in 'The Eastern Aboretum' by James Grigor as 'a delightful garden with a profusion of sylvan ornaments, among some of the finest trees including the Cedar of Lebanon'.

Plate 68c   *Year 1995*

In 1948 Mr Priest sold the property to Mr E. E. Hines, also a Norwich engineer, but he retained for his own use the adjacent small gamekeeper's cottage (69) and then moved to Costessey Lodge (113). Mr Hines died in 1975 and his widow died a few months later. The property is now owned by their younger daughter, Isobel, who has turned some of the rooms into convenient flats for paying guests.

When Woodside Cottage, now Eastwood Lodge, was used as a vicarage, the route taken to church was up and over Greenhills Wood to The Croft, then across the road to and through Money's Hills to Sandy Lane, now Folgate Lane, via a gateway in the hedge opposite the present day Sidney Road. This gate existed up to 1955 but because the Rev. William Tretheway (1945-1963) still made use of this now private rear entrance to Silver Springs as a short cut to The Croft, the gate was removed, the hedge reinstated, and a new rear entrance made. A gateway for a similar short cut to Folgate Lane is mentioned in section (62).

69

Gamekeeper's Cottage
Townhouse Road
T. 449

This little cottage adjacent to the western side of Woodside Cottage (68) was used as accommodation for the general gamekeepers or other employees of the Costessey Estate, although in the Tithe Award of 1840 it was occupied by Richard Spaul, a shoemaker, and he was followed in about 1870 by P. Simmons, when it was known as Simmons Cottage.

About 1900 Mr Arthurton (plate 69b), a gamekeeper, was the occupier. He was followed by Mr E. Denny, an employee of Costessey Estate who was the occupier at the time of the Costessey Estate sale in 1918 in which it was described as a Keepers' Cottage, well built in brick with a thatched roof, and having two rooms downstairs and two rooms upstairs. In this small cottage Mrs Denny brought up their three daughters and their one

Plate 69a

Year 1918

Plate 69b

Plate 69c   Year 1904

son, whose death in the First World War upset the balance of Mrs Denny's mind and she had to be taken into care. This cottage, then known as Denny's Cottage, was included with Woodside Cottage in the 1918 sale, and was bought by Mr A. E. Priest.

On selling Woodside Cottage (68) to Mr E.E. Hines, the little Denny's Cottage was retained by Mr Priest, but it became very dilapidated after the Second World War, and, during a heavy storm in the 1950s, the thatch was stripped off making it necessary to cover the roof with a large tarpaulin.

After the death of Mr Priest at Costessey Lodge (113) his widow returned to Denny's Cottage in 1959 and, after having it demolished, had a bungalow (plate 69d) built on the site for her own accommodation. The property is now owned by her grand-daughter, Juliet Hall who, with her husband, has renovated it into a modern chalet.

Plate 69d

70
Greenhills Wood
T.509 and T.511

This wood, owned by the Costessey Estate, was known as Coney Hills in the Manorial Records of 1587, and has always been accessible to the public, with footpaths leading from Townhouse Road to The Croft. When the Rev. Thomas Watson and the Rev. James Evans used Woodside Cottage their route to church took them up through these woods (68).

At the Costessey Estate sale the wood was withdrawn but was later bought by Mr Stanley Howes, a motor engineer of Norwich, who carried on the public access facilities. On his death in 1961, his widow, Mrs Violet Howes (31), succeeded and in 1963 sold Greenhills Wood to the Forestry Commission for a peppercorn payment of one shilling on the understanding that they would maintain the wood and ensure that the public access would always exist. This they did until 1983 when, due to government restrictions on forestry grants, they were forced to sell many woods, with Greenhills Wood being one of them.

Although the 1963 sale contained a clause that, should the Commission decide to sell, it would sell back to Mrs Howes at the same peppercorn rate, this clause was proved to have no legal binding and the wood was offered for sale on the open market for £12,000. In 1985 the Costessey Parish Council became the new owners at the agreed price, and to celebrate the transfer of ownership, a handing over ceremony of the deeds was arranged. A short service took place around a specially planted tree with the Rev. John Bourne and Father Richard Wilson each bestowing his own ecclesiastical benediction on to the tree, with a hope for a vigorous future growth.

However, the disastrous gale of 1987 bestowed its own type of benediction on the tree and promptly uprooted it, and, as with other trees around, it was cleared away by the contractors.

Plate 70   *Year 1909*

71

Beech Cottage, Townhouse Road

T.215

These semi-detached cottages were built by Thomas Kidd between 1834 and 1836 and he is the recorded owner in the 1840 Tithe Award, with Robert Fox and Henry Baker as tenants. After the death of Thomas Kidd in 1864, the cottages were sold to the Costessey Estate, and at the 1918 sale they were sold to R. H. Tebb from London, the tenants at this time being S. Dann and a Mr Fisher. Mr Tebb sold them to a general dealer named Drake. At this time a Mrs Laws was a tenant with other tenants being, James Fuller, an estate carpenter, George Flatman, an allotment holder who also ran a pony and cart transport service, and a Mr George Fisher.

In March 1949, Miss Margery Lewis, an employee of the Norfolk County Council, became the owner and lived in one of the cottages with Mr George Fisher still remaining as tenant in the next door cottage, and when this became vacant the whole building was internally modernised and converted into one single dwelling with Miss Lewis being joined in the accommodation by Miss Amy Bates (10).

Plate 71

72
Council Houses, Townhouse Road
T.217

The strip of land on which the above council houses now stand was, in 1840, known as Field's Pyghtle and was owned by Thomas Kidd. It was arable land and worked by George King, a gardener. After the death of Thomas Kidd in 1864, his grandson sold the property, which included Beech Cottage (71) and The Old Forge (73) together with a cottage and a barn, to the Costessey Estate. This again made it necessary for the Estate to raise the money required by mortgage, and, as often was the case, more than one mortgagor was involved in raising the required amount.

In 1894 The Housing of the Working Classes Act 1890 -1909 came into being, under which local councils were obliged to provide houses for the working classes. As practically all the conveniently located land available for such houses was owned by the Costessey Estate, no building of this type could immediately take place. However, on the death of the last

Plate 72a

Plate 72b   *Year 1985*

Plate 72c   *Year 1990*

Lord Stafford at Costessey Hall in 1913 and the imminent sale of the Costessey Estate, the Forehoe R.D.C. decided to act in advance of any impending sale and acquire this strip of land which, at this time, was worked by Frederick Barnes, a gardener. He put in a claim for compensation if he was to be turned off this field, and this was settled in June 1914 when he agreed to accept five pounds in full settlement.

Because of the number of mortgagors involved, the purchase of this piece of land by the Forehoe R.D.C. became very protracted, and it was not until October 1915 that the deeds and documents were received. The cost of the land on which to build these three pairs of semi-detached houses was £70 but, with compensation and proportioned rent with interest, the total cost became £91. 13. 9. The houses were reputed to have been some of the first council houses to be built in Norfolk. In the 1960s these houses were updated and the original large gardens taken over for infill houses making a total of twelve council houses on this site.

73
Forge Cottage and Garage
Townhouse Road
T.216

At the western end of Field's Pyghtle was the old forge cottage and barn, all owned in 1840 by Thomas Kidd, with the forge being used by him for his building business. He gave up his building business shortly before his death and let the forge to William Gooderson who made and sold farming machines. Standing a little further back on this site were, in 1840, two cottages owned and, almost without doubt, built by Thomas Kidd. In 1840 they were occupied by William Harvey and William Barnes whose son, Frederick, worked the adjoining field (72).

At the 1918 sale of Costessey Estate the old forge and the two cottages and barn were put up for sale but did not reach the reserve figure and were withdrawn. Charles Dunnell, a motor engineer who already had a small garage in White Hart Plain adjoining the old blacksmiths' shop

Plate 73

(78), decided to buy the old forge property with the two cottages at the rear, occupied at this time by Mr Goldsmith and Mrs Barnes, her husband, Frederick, having died about 1917.

Charles Dunnell demolished the old barn and on the site built a garage which became known as Townhouse Road Garage. He died about 1946 leaving the property to his wife. The forge was let to Mr Codling, a blacksmith and small builder, whilst the garage was let to Messrs Reynolds and Hostler.

After the death of Mrs Dunnell in about 1958, the property was sold and eventually the forge and cottages became owned by Charles Allison of Taverham who was a tractor owner and small builder. He made considerable alterations to the two cottages bringing them up to modern standards. Unfortunately, he tragically lost his life at an early age, but his widow, Elizabeth Allison, remained living in one of the renovated cottages with her son, David, occupying the adjoining cottage.

After the death of Mr Hostler, Mr Reynolds left the garage, which was then acquired by Edward Took and Raymond Smith who ran the business as Townhouse Coachworks, specializing in the rebuilding of classic and vintage cars, a business that came to an abrupt end on Whit Monday 1974 when it was destroyed by fire. Mr Harry Serruys, a Norwich business man who lost two of his vintage cars in the fire, became the next owner, and in March 1987 sold out to Glynn Webster who now runs the business as W.C.S. Townhouse Coachworks, Old Costessey.

74
Parish Hall
Townhouse Road
T.51

The 1840 Tithe Award lists John Clarke as the owner of the land on which the Parish Hall now stands. In about 1846 he sold the land to the Costessey Estate as parish records state that the Costessey Estate gave this piece of land on which to build, at that time, a reading room. This was completed in 1902, the vicar of Costessey, the Rev. John Hampson, being very prominent in raising public subscriptions for it to be built. A few years later the Rev. Hampson obtained a grant for an extension to the reading room for a public library. The Parish Council had agreed to adopt the new Libraries Act which allowed a small amount to be taken from the rates for the purchase of books. In 1907 the extension to the east side of the hall was completed.

In the 1920s the Norfolk County Council adopted the Libraries Act for all Norfolk, towards which service every parish had to pay and shortly after this the Costessey public library closed but the Reading Room remained as a recreational venue. However, over the years interest dwindled and it was very little used.

The west gable-end had caused some earlier trouble and expense due to brickwork cracking, said to be caused by faulty foundations. The buttresses, then built against this wall and the adjacent front window, solved this problem.

Today, the Parish Hall is extensively used by the Parish Council and also by many local clubs and societies, with the old public library room now being used as office accommodation for the police.

Plate 74

75

St Walstan's Roman Catholic Church
Townhouse Road
T.196 and T.197

The land on which this church now stands was originally part of Parkhouse Farm (80) owned by the Costessey Estate and occupied in 1834 by Robert Fox who agreed to vacate this small part of the farm. The Rev. Dr Husenbeth had raised sufficient funds and in 1834 the building of the church commenced but available funds soon ran out and work came to a standstill. An article appeared in the 'Catholic Magazine' of March 1835 which stated, 'Only the exterior of the church has been completed but windows are not yet glazed. A considerable sum of money will be needed to finish off the interior and build a presbytery. Unless some charitable benefactor comes along, this beautiful edifice must be abandoned to the bats and the owls'. Work did start again but with a few more temporary stoppages due to lack of funds. However, completion was achieved by 1841.

In 1871 Sir Henry Valentine Stafford Jerningham, Lord Stafford, made over to the Rev. Husenbeth as a Deed of Gift, the church land and all buildings standing on it. One year later the Rev. Husenbeth died, and Lord Stafford's chaplain, Mgr G. Davis, refused to take services at the church. Apart from funerals, the church was closed for the next twenty-four years, during which time the presbytery was let out to Mr Rackham and then to Daniel Brett, a corn merchant of Norwich.

On the appointment of The Very Rev. Thomas, Canon Fitzgerald in December 1896, the Presbytery was re-conditioned and he took up residence here. He then turned his attention to the poor state of the interior of the church caused by twenty-four years of closure. In 1909 Canon Fitzgerald arranged, at his own expense, for a group of London orphans to spend a short holiday in Costessey, and photograph (plate 75c) shows them at the ford (plate 119c) in Longwater Lane. It was 1910, when the Rev. Byrne succeeded Canon Fitzgerald, before the church was back to full parochial use as it still is today with Father Richard Wilson in charge.

Plate 75a   *Year 1951*

Plate 75b   *Year 1909*

Plate 75c   *Year 1909*

149

76

White Hart Public House

T. 52

At the junction of The Street, West End and Townhouse Road is an area known in the past as White Hart Plain. Photograph (76a) shows this area as it was in 1880 and is the only one that can be traced which shows the old building, on the extreme right, in which the first Costessey Post Office was opened (77). On the extreme left is the old blacksmith's shop and house, and this would be well before the first village shop was opened here (78). In the centre of the photograph is the old White Hart of which the first mention in the Manorial Records was in 1698 when Peter Hunt bought, from James Rippon and Sarah Roper, property that may have been an earlier White Hart.

In 1819, John Burgis became the owner of this earlier property and it is almost without doubt that he pulled the old White Hart down and, about 1830, built this White Hart of which the first mention was at the Manorial Court in1839 when John Burgis sold it to John Clarke, with James Miller as the tenant. He had previously been the tenant of the White Swan, just along The Street (3), but by 1845 James Miller had left the White Hart and returned to the White Swan. John Clarke then took over as 'Mine Host' at his own White Hart, but in 1846 he sold it to Richard Bullard, Brewers of Norwich. Charles Banham is listed as the tenant of the White Hart in 1864.

In the 1880s when James Yallop, a canary breeder from Norwich, took over as tenant, a local farm labourers' union was formed with its headquarters at the White Hart. This, however, only lasted for a few years as it refused to amalgamate with the newly formed main body. James Yallop left to take up farming but failed and returned to canary breeding. About six more tenants came and departed during which time a Tradesmen's Club was formed with its headquarters at the White Hart but, in the early 1900s, it also ceased. Also a branch of the East Anglian Oddfellows had its headquarters here, but it also ceased just after the 1911 Health Insurance Act became law.

Between the White Hart and the Reading Room (plate 76b) was a double fronted cart-shed containing a manger and hay rack for horses when their owners were inside the White Hart. Later on it was used as a shelter by

Plate 76a   *Year 1890*

Plate 76b   *Year 1902*

151

Plate 76c   *Year 1950*

passengers waiting for the newly formed United Bus Service to Norwich and much resentment was felt when it was demolished in 1930 for the building of the present day White Hart which was completed in 1931 with Mr E. Fenwick as the new tenant. In the 1960s, during the tenancy of Frederick Copley, the old property next door known as Hart House (3) was demolished in order to make a larger car park and to build a Function Room.

The White Hart is now owned by Inntrepreneur but at the present time managers stay for only short periods before moving to other licensed premises. Graham Cole was the manager in the early 1996s but has now left and Pedro and staff have taken over.

77
The Two Old Post Offices
Townhouse Road
T.53 and T. 402

Immediately to the right and to the front of the old White Hart (plate 76a) is an old building shown on the 1880 Ordnance Survey map as a post office (plate 1a). In the 1840 Tithe Award, John Clarke who bought the old White Hart in 1839 is listed as the owner with Thomas Stone as the occupier. Following Thomas Stone, John Spaul, a tailor (95), moved in and soon became the first postmaster. Letters came in from Norwich by foot arriving at 10 a.m. each day, with the post office business being conducted in the living room. John Spaul died in 1864, and his son, Caius, took over until 1897. In 1898 the Costessey Estate built a new post office on the opposite side of the roadwith John Laws, an Estate worker, moving in as the new postmaster (plate 77a). The old post office building across the road was then demolished and, by 1902, the Reading Room, later to be known as the Parish Hall, was built (plate 76b).

Plate 77a   *Year 1907*

Plate 77b   *Year 1920*   *Plate 77c*   *Year 1920*

Plate 77d   *Year 1920*

Plate 77e   *Year 1951*

Plate 77f   *Year 1995*

John Laws, the first postmaster in the new post office, died in 1903 and his son, also John, took over. He proved a most unsatisfactory postmaster and was replaced in 1906 by Francis Welch from Norwich. He started up a shop in the post office and became an enthusiastic amateur photographer building himself a light-proof brick shed, seen at the extreme left (plate 77d). He is seen leaning against the post office wall during a Christmas postal rush (plate 77c). At this time the post came in from Norwich by pony and cart seen in the background of (plate 77a). Mr Welch died in 1942 at the age of 66 after which his entire stock of old negatives was lost, but many of his old photographs were available as postcards and a good selection of these have now been found and used in this record.

The post office was also used as the Telephone Exchange in the early part of the 1900s, having a small switchboard installed in a back room by the National Telephone Company. In 1911 the General Post Office (GPO) took over all telephone companies under the control of the Post Office Engineering Dept, and an early post office engineer is seen on maintenance work at the old switchboard which could handle about fifteen subscribers (plate 77b). In the early 1930s a new telephone exchange was built in The Street (7). By 1950 the small lean-to shop (plate 77d) was inadequate for the increasing business and a second lean-to was built facing the original shop but this valley-type roof did not meet with official approval and the two roof ridges were connected to form a flat roof. This new roof soon had maintenance problems and a hipped roof was finally built.

After the death of Francis Welch, his widow, Margaret, took over and remained until her death in 1963 when her daughter-in-law, Janet Welch, took over, during which time the Postal and Telephone sections of the GPO became separate organisations and the telephone kiosk had to be removed from the forecourt of the post office. A suitable site was found against the front of the Parish Hall.

By 1990, owing to the ill health of Janet Welch, the post office was closed and the business transferred to the Hart Stores (78) under the management of Maurice and Barbara Houldsworth. The old post office is now in use again by Mr W. Hinton, who has opened up a shop under the name 'Townhouse Pine'.

78
Hart Stores and Blacksmiths' Shop
White Hart Plain
T.445

The 1840 Tithe Award shows that the house, now Costessey Post Office, and the blacksmiths' shop were both owned by the Costessey Estate. The first mention of this property was at the Manorial Court when John Graver succeeded his father in accordance with his father's will which clearly stated that John must not sell nor mortgage the property. If John could not do this, his brother, Robert, could when he took over in1752, and, by 1759, Robert had got further into debt and sold the property to the Costessey Estate.

In 1840 John Spaul was the occupying blacksmith and had been here for a number of years. He made the entrance gates for both the Roman Catholic Church and St Edmund's Church in Costessey. On his death in 1856 his nephew, also John Spaul, took over the blacksmiths' business which, in 1880, was taken over by his son-in-law, Frederick Gunton, a builder. He then employed two men to work as blacksmiths whilst he renovated and re-

Plate 78a   *Year 1920*

157

roofed the adjacent house, after which he and his wife moved in as tenants of the Costessey Estate, and in the 1918 Estate sale the house and shop were listed as being let to Mrs F.Gunton whilst the blacksmiths' shop was let to Mr F. Gunton.

In the 1890s Charles Dunnell, an engineer, built himself a small timber and glass- fronted garage on the eastern end of the blacksmiths' shop (plate 78a). However, in the 1918 sale all this property was put under one lot and was bought by Frederick Gunton.Charles Dunnell had anticipated this and had previously bought the Old Forge (73).Frederick Gunton died in 1925 and his property was bought by William Squires who demolished the old blacksmiths' shop and Dunnell's garage and built two cottages on the cleared site where two forges had been working for a few hundred years.

Mr Squires sold out to George Harwood who continued the grocery shop started up by Mrs Gunton. David Francis became the next owner until he sold out to Adrian and Sylvia Blyth who, owing to health reasons, sold out to Maurice and Barbara Houldsworth. After enlarging the shop in1990, they took over the Post Office counter services for Old Costessey, and in1995 they introduced a newsagency department. It is now known as Hart Stores and Post Office. Photograph (78b) shows how it was in 1958. Note Costessey Hall tower, known as the Thornbury Tower, in the central distance. This tower partially collapsed in the 1970s after which it was demolished.

Plate 78b   *Year 1958*

Plate 78c   *Year 1914*

Plate 78d   *Year 1992*

159

79
Ivy Cottage, 12 West End
T. 394

As this cottage was freehold up to the time that it was acquired by the Costessey Estate, very little of its past history is known. The 1840 Tithe Award lists the Costessey Estate as the owner and William Cole, a wheelwright, as a tenant. He had a workshop at the western end of the cottage. In the 1880s he was followed by his son, Charles, also a wheelwright (100). In 1889 the Costessey Estate renovated the cottage and re-roofed it after increasing the number of bedrooms to four. William Gunton then became the new tenant. After a few years at the cottage, Mr Gunton, at his own expense, added a bathroom over a lean-to scullery at the rear. For this the Estate allowed him a year's free rent. He moved from Ivy Cottage in about 1903 to Wensum Cottage (33), and Mr H. J. Thompson, of Costessey Mill (53), moved in.

At the Costessey Estate sale in 1918, Ivy Cottage was withdrawn at £475 but sold later to Michael Blake. It was then let to tenants including the Rev. Burton, the retired vicar of Litcham, Norfolk, who, on his death, was taken back to Litcham for burial. His widow remained at Ivy Cottage until her death in 1960. George Wade then became owner and he was followed by Dr. Knights who organised a number of garden parties during his short stay here. Tony Loveday, a senior police officer, was the next owner until 1987 when he sold out to Nigel Rust, a designer of TV stage sets.

Plate 79　　　　　　　　　　　　　　　　　　　　*Year 1918*

80
Aerial Photograph
Parkhouse Farm and Abattoir
West End
T.403 and T.405

Situated in the centre of the village and having long frontages to Townhouse Road, West End and Longwater Lane was the old Parkhouse Farm (plate 80b), owned by the Costessey Estate and, in 1840, occupied by Edmund Martin, the owner of Costessey windmill (64). When he left the farm it was taken over by The Hon. Francis Jerningham, a brother of Sir Henry Valentine Stafford Jerningham, Lord Stafford of Costessey Hall. The Hon. Francis Jerningham acted mainly as agent for the Costessey Estate.

Joseph Harris was the next occupier of Parkhouse Farm but turned out to be a very poor farmer and left about 1902 to take over Church Farm (48). The next occupiers were Messrs Dann and Son. Steven Dann had a milk round and also sold milk straight from the farm dairy. This he carried on until the 1918 sale of the Costessey Estate in which a buyer could not be found. Parts of the farm were then sold up for building development.

Plate 80a

Plate 80b   *Year 1951*

Plate 80c

Plate 80d
Year 1993

163

John Hewitt then bought the rest of the farm and lived here until 1935 when John Blake, a Norwich speculator, bought it and sold more land for building development. He then installed his son, Hilton, in the farmhouse and obtained a slaughter licence. There was much opposition in the village to this because of the nearness of the school and the likelihood that drainage from the slaughter-house to a meadow across the road would be offensive As all sanitary conditions were complied with, the opposition failed and up to 1994 a large business was carried on (plate 80c). However, in common with other abattoirs in Britain, Blake's abattoir had to be improved to meet the E.E.C. regulations, otherwise it would be forced to close. An alternative site for a modern abattoir was found on the outskirts of Felthorpe and by 1995 Blake's abattoir at Costessey had closed.

The old farmhouse and the barns of the old Parkhouse Farm seen at the near top on the right of the aerial photograph (plate 80b) have now been completely demolished, and the site developed with housing by Wimpey Builders.

81
S. and G. Sergent, Engineers Ltd
West End
T. 604a

S. and G. Sergent Engineers Ltd started up, in 1949, as a small engineering firm in The Street, Costessey just north of the shop (4). Advertising brought in more work than could be handled in a small workshop, so a move to larger premises at the junction of Longwater Lane with West End opposite the school was made (85). Trade still increased and there was a search for an even larger site. It was found in West End opposite the Parkfarm Abattoir (80). This site was owned by H. G. Blake who agreed to sell to Sergents, and in 1962 a planning application was submitted by Sergents to erect an engineering workshop here.

A great deal of local opposition was generated against this application and, although the Norfolk County Council supported the proposals, local

Plate 81a

Year 1969

opposition was such that, in August 1962, the Ministry of Housing and Local Government intervened and permission was granted.

Business again increased (plate 81a) and, as members of the Export Merchants' Association, they hosted a 'Down Your Way' BBC broadcast with Brian Johnston on the 4th October 1967. Later, in July 1969, they were awarded the 'Gold Award' by the International Export Association which was presented to Stanley and Geoffrey Sergent by Robert Green, Parish Council Chairman (plate 81b) and farmer of Bridge Farm (116).

Business continued well for a number of years until the trade recession set in during the early 1980s. S. and G. Sergent decided to sell up but no buyer could be found and, like many other small engineering firms, they were forced to sell their expensive equipment for scrap value. The Gold Award flag (plate 81b) was unceremoniously dumped by Mrs Phillips, far left foreground (plate 81b), much to the dismay of the Sergent brothers. Shortly afterwards Mrs Phillips, who lived in the old Red Lion (94), emigrated to Australia. After all the equipment had been removed, the empty building was sold to Robert Thompson who then opened up the West End Cue Club.

Plate 81b   *Year 1969*

82
Wensum Motors, West End Garage
28 West End – T.407

Before the turn of the 19th century there was a belt of magnificent beech trees bordering the road at this part of West End when Edmund Martin was the tenant farmer of Parkhouse Farm (80). After the farm was again put up for sale in 1919, parts of the land were sold separately and Mr F. Cribb bought a piece next door to Rose Cottage (84) on which he built his garage and repair shop. He then travelled down to Southampton Docks to buy one of the old ambulances being brought back to England from the First World War. After driving this back to Costessey, he converted it into a public service bus and started up a motor transport service to Norwich which put an end to the pony and cart service.

About 1925 Mr Cribb attracted competition from the newly formed United Bus Company who ran a service to Norwich free of charge, and Mr Cribb's service was abandoned, after which the United Bus Company started charging fares. He sold out about 1930 to Mr H.Cann who, in 1950, built a house on the site and opened up a petrol station and repair shop for motor cars, selling out in the 1960s to two motor mechanic brothers. They carried on the repair and servicing business under the name of Wensum Motors, building a retail shop for car and cycle accessories. They sold out after a few years and other owners took over including one dealing in fishing tackle. Eventually the property was taken over by Roger G. Anderson. The petrol pumps were removed and the business is now concerned with the repair and rebuilding of motorised caravans.

Plate 82

167

83
The Catholic School
19 West End
T.444

At the request of Lady Jerningham, Sir George Jerningham, 7th Baronet, was obliged to build a school to educate the Roman Catholic children of Costessey. It would also be built at the entire expense of Sir George. A piece of land was allocated from Parkhouse Farm at the junction of Longwater Lane and West End, and by 1821 the school was completed.

The first teacher was Thomas Roulston and the method of teaching was known as the Lancastrian method in which more advanced pupils helped with the early teaching of the younger pupils. In 1856 the schoolhouse was built and the first occupiers were Mr and Mrs Charles Smith who, in 1850, had replaced Mr Roulston.

The Education Act came into force in 1870 when the lay teachers were replaced by more qualified staff, and Mrs Beresford and her son, Mr A. Beresford, became the new teachers until about 1872 when their places were taken by two nuns, Sisters of Charity from St Paul's Convent, Selly Park, Birmingham. They left after a year or two to gain more experience. Thomas Roulston returned to cover the teaching period to 1877 when the nuns returned to start a hundred years of teaching at this school. They took up residence in the schoolhouse which then became known as The Convent.

About 1890, the school was enlarged, with further extensions in 1959 to accommodate the increasing number of children, now of all religious persuasions. The nuns finally left the school in 1976 and the school then became known as St Augustine's Primary School with Mrs Hogg becoming the first headmistress under the new administration. Mrs Hogg held this position until her retirement in August 1995, to be followed by Mr Paul George in September 1995.

The convent closed in 1977, the building being transferred to secular use, namely as a youth centre and retreat. It was also used by the Catholic parish as a meeting venue for various activities. However, it was found not to be a financial success and in 1983 was put on the market for sale. Very little interest was shown, so the building was finally auctioned in September 1983 and was bought by Mr Reg. Piesse, a retired lecturer, lay preacher and Parish Councillor.

Plate 83a
Year 1920

Plate 83b
Year 1970

Plate 83c

84
Rose Cottage
32 West End
T.337

In 1820 when the Rev Dr Frederick Charles Husenbeth arrived in Costessey to become priest at Costessey Hall, he declined the invitation to take up residence at the Hall, much preferring to find accommodation in the village. Situated in the centre of the village and opposite Longwater Lane was a freehold residence owned by the Costessey Estate and known as Rose Cottage. This he chose as his residence. During his time at Rose Cottage he used a room at the rear of the building as a Roman Catholic Chapel. He bathed every morning in a pond behind the house and became a familiar thickset figure as he visited his parishioners, which on Fridays were timed to coincide with the midday meal so as to ensure abstinence from meat . He remained here until the new church and presbytery were completed in 1841. Thomas Craggs, a groom and confidential servant to Lord Stafford, was the next occupier but by 1864 Alfred Willsea Barber was the listed tenant after which Monsignor Davis moved in around 1874. Although he resigned his chaplaincy at the Hall in 1896, he was allowed to remain at Rose Cottage until his death in 1911.

During the First World War, Rose Cottage was taken over by the War Department and used as accommodation for wives of regimental officers stationed at Costessey Hall. Rose Cottage was next occupied by Paul J. Lambert at a rent of £25 per annum. He was a Norwich tea merchant but it seems that at times he was so under the influence of alcohol that, according to village gossip, he was paid to keep away from the firm's Norwich office. At the 1918 sale of Costessey Estate, Rose Cottage was withdrawn at £500.

In 1931 the Rev. Thomas Culter Des-Barres was appointed vicar of Colney and, on his retirement in 1938, moved to Costessey and took up residence at Rose Cottage by which time the single front entrance gate had been changed to a double gate. He remained here until his death in 1948 when his wife succeeded him. He is seen in photograph (84) standing in his front garden. His wife died in 1952 and left the property to her two

Plate 84   *Year 1938*

nieces who, in October 1952, sold out to John F. Olorenshaw, a director of a Norwich motor business. He made a number of alterations to the entrance to allow motor access. In April 1983 he sold out to Mr John Brown, a director of Bernard Matthews, plc.

85
Aerial Photograph

This aerial photograph, taken in 1951, shows at the bottom right hand corner, Mr Cann's black-roofed garage (plate 82) with Rose Cottage next to it. Lower left is the Roman Catholic school (83). Notice that the old playground shelter, built in 1902 and known as the Drill Hall, is still standing, but, shortly after this photograph was taken, the timber stanchions supporting the heavy tiled roof began to fail which produced a five inch list out of vertical, making it necessary to prop it up. Offered up for sale it attracted no buyers so, becoming a danger to the children, it was demolished, as were the children's old toilets, centre bottom.

Above the school and on the other side of Longwater Lane is the old engineering workshop of S. and G. Sergent (81). This had been acquired from Sissen and Bugdale who had set up a builders' business about 1925. They built many low-priced houses and bungalows in New Costessey but, shortly after the Second World War, the business failed.

Next to Rose Cottage and partially hidden by trees, is a pair of semi-detached cottages (86). Further up West End and close to the roadside, is a row of very small cottages known as Birdcage Row (88) and almost opposite these is the cottage known previously as White Cottages (87). The last house, clearly seen with its roadside gable-end to West End, was known as Falcon Close (91). Butting up to the left side walls of the school is the old school house built in 1856 (83). In 1877 it became the Convent for the nuns who were then teachers at the school, but in 1977 it reverted to secular use until becoming a private residence in 1983 (plate 83c).

Plate 85

Year 1951

86
Riverside Cottages
36 West End
T.193

This pair of semi-detached cottages was formerly one single dwelling and was owned up to 1702 by Ralph Belward when he sold it to Lockyer Byer. By 1822 Edward Hastings had taken it over by the will of his mother. He was a master carpenter, employing men who worked on carpentry for the Costessey Hall extension, the Roman Catholic church and the Presbytery for which they made many special wooden moulds for the very intricate brickwork required for these buildings.

However, financial difficulties forced him to mortgage his property and in 1868 it was sold to the Costessey Estate, with his daughter, Dominica Hastings, remaining as tenant. She carried on a small private school for 'genteel young ladies' until the 1890s after which the house was divided into two cottages, under the name of Riverside Cottages.

Miss Hastings died in 1916 thus ending a long association with the Hastings family in Costessey since 1786. At the Costessey Estate sale in 1918 the tenants were Mrs Melton, who died in 1952 at the age of 93, and Mr A. White, bringing in a combined rent of £10 per annum. The property was bought at the sale by Edward Hardingham for £260.

In 1974 the larger of the two cottages was bought at an auction by Leslie R. Draper, a builder, and the smaller cottage was acquired by Mr Olorenshaw who owned Rose Cottage (84), the adjacent property. The smaller cottage was then let out to various tenants for at least the next twelve years until it was sold to Beryl Willis. On her departure from Costessey in 1994 she sold out to Mr Draper who has now brought the two cottages back into one single dwelling.

Plate 86

87
The White Cottages
25 - 27 West End
T.548

These cottages were first mentioned at the Manorial Court in 1756. However, they go back much further as, in a survey in 1951 by Col. Glendenning, a 16th century window of five lights using moulding that was in vogue between 1550 and 1620 was identified. About 1650 the roof was raised to create a three-storey building. It was thatched and had the usual Tudor stepped gable ends. This property is assumed to have been the old Red Lion beer house as in October 1756 when Robert French lived here, he applied to the Manorial Court for permission to enclose a piece of waste land between Longwater Lane and his boundary of the Red Lion beer house.

After the death of Robert French the old Red Lion was taken over by Robert Fox, and about this time in the late 1700s the building must have closed as a beer house with the name being transferred to the beer house further along West End (94). Robert Fox died in 1829, the property being acquired by the Costessey Estate who then turned it into three separate cottages for tenants. One tenant was William Spaul, a boot and shoe repairer but, after he caught a severe attack of influenza in 1895, he hanged himself in one of his sheds.

In 1912 the previously raised roof was demolished by the Costessey Estate and the whole building renovated to more modern standards after which three new tenants moved in, W. Hostler, Robert Blake and J. Barnes. At the 1918 sale of Costessey Estate, the property was sold to R. H. Tebb for £300. It was then sold to Mrs E. Carr who carried out further renovations. In the early 1950s the cottage with the gable end (plate 87c) towards the roadway was demolished reducing the property to a pair of semi-detached cottages. They are still in the Carr family with Colin Carr at number 25 and Edward Carr at number 27 West End.

Plate 87a   *Year 1900*

Plate 87b   *Year 1930*

Plate 87c   *Year 1918*

88
Birdcage Row, West End
T.195

Birdcage Row was a row of six very small cottages, seen almost centrally on the aerial photograph (85). These cottages were owned in 1840 by William Hastings who, being a builder, most probably built them on about a quarter of an acre of land. At this time there were only five cottages with tenants John Hastings, James Morter, John Drake, William Friar and John Hostler. The sixth cottage was squeezed in on the west end of the row in the later 1880s. Each cottage had one room and a scullery downstairs with one room and a small box room upstairs and, hanging outside in fair weather, most tenants had a bird in a cage. A communal toilet block was situated at the rear of the row.

Many young couples started up their married life in Birdcage Row until something better came their way, and quite a few families, behind in rent on larger cottages, were moved into these smaller cottages.

When upgrading of sanitary conditions began to be enforced by law, these cottages which were slowly becoming slums were a problem and, after 1920, the owner was compelled to turn the six cottages into three larger cottages. This he did but the three occupying tenants promptly sublet the extra rooms and Birdcage Row reverted to its original condition, much to the disgust of the Costessey Parish Council.

Some of the occupiers at this period were F. Cribb (82), Walter Cousins, a postman, Robert Cousins and Ernest Bishop who, on Sunday mornings, would turn his room into a barber's shop. He was not a very good barber pulling out more hair than he cut, but, once he had made enough ready cash, he would close his barber's shop and make a quick dash in the direction of the White Hart. He has been reported to have gone out of his mind just before his death and, divesting himself of all his clothes, ran naked through the street of West End. Directly behind Birdcage Row was a row of three larger cottages the entrance to which was against the west end of Birdcage Row where the cap-headed lady is standing (plate 88).

Plate 88   *Year 1910*

During the Second World War the cottages were used for evacuees, but after the war the first chance of demolition was taken. On the extreme right of photograph (88) is part of the old Red Lion (87), later known as the White Cottages, now 25 - 27 West End.

89

Lion Cottages, 37 West End
T.326 and T.328

Although the cottages on this site have been traced back to 1564, the first mention of them in the Manorial Court was in April 1829 when the executors of Robert Fox who had bought them in 1809, sold them to the Costessey Estate. At this period they were occupied by Christina Grant and for a number of years the cottages were known as Grant's Cottages. In the 1840 Tithe Award, the occupiers are listed as Joseph Grant and John Finnerly. Joseph Grant was a glass stainer and produced some of the stained glass that filled the narrow lancet windows of the Roman Catholic Church. Other tenants followed including George Carr, Alfred Wilkinson, James Simmons and Joseph High.

At the 1918 sale of the Costessey Estate, the tenants were C. Doggett and H. Josiah, the cottages being bought by a property speculator, Mr Crabb, for £170. At this time, the double-fronted building had one single porch entrance opening on to two porches dividing the building into two dwellings (plate 89a). The property then became owned by the Blake family with Mr and Mrs Blake (senior) living in the east side and their son, Maurice, with his son, Maurice, occupying the west side. On the death of Mrs Blake (senior) the east side cottage was let to Mr Ireson, he being followed by Sheila Howes. She then moved out about 1956 when the two cottages were converted into one dwelling.

 In 1971 the building was completely renovated with the top front windows reglazed and the old central entrance porch demolished. A new side entrance was provided with all work carried out under the strict supervision of the architect, Mr David Porritt. Maurice Blake moved back into the renovated cottage and remained here until 1977, followed by Dr T. Whitehead, Dr Barclay and Mr and Mrs Roe. In 1988 the property was sold to John and Diana Green, electrical contractors.

Photograph (89b/90) taken outside Lion Cottages is of C. H. Cannell, a coal and coke merchant. He used to take his pony and dray through the ford (54) and on to Drayton railway station where he would collect his load of coal and coke for sale in Costessey. Notice the old spelling of 'Cossey' still being used colloquially on the headboard of his dray.

90
Park Cottage and Knott Cottage
45 - 47 West End
T.329

The old property standing on this site was also owned by Robert Fox and, like Lion Cottages next door, was sold in 1829 to the Costessey Estate. In 1840 the occupier of the old building was George Grant, a carpenter, but soon after this period the Costessey Estate demolished the old building and built a pair of semi-detached cottages in its place with a frontal red-brick porch serving both properties. These were let to Estate workers such as William White, an Estate carpenter and local rate collector. Next door to him was Samuel Gregory who then lived here for a good number of years. Like most property built by the Estate the brick chimneys were of ornamental design.

At the 1918 sale of Costessey Estate these semi-detached cottages were bought by Mr Bartlett with William Markwell and Jack Carr as tenants. Park Cottage

Plate 89a   *Year 1918*

181

Plate 89b, 90   *Year 1920*

has been unoccupied for a few years, the owner not wishing to sell. Knott Cottage next door, which has an interesting brickwork shield from Costessey Hall built into a wall, is owned by Mr G. Davison. These cottages are seen far right on photograph (89b/90).

91

Falcon Close, 53 West End

T.327, T. 443 and T. 576a

The cottages on this site appear to be some of the oldest in Costessey and were first mentioned in the Manorial Court in 1681 when Andrew Hanner sold the rear cottage of the three to Ann Moore. Passing down through various owners they came under the ownership of Robert Fox in 1823 and, once again, his executors sold out to the Costessey Estate in 1829.

The Tithe Award of 1840 lists William Pank as occupying the cottage at the rear, whilst the roadside cottage was occupied by Jacob Frosdick. By 1880 the rear cottage had been demolished, and the roadside cottage converted into two cottages with one room upstairs and one room downstairs each with its own individual staircase. A Costessey police constable occupied one cottage and when he moved out William Pank moved in from the rear cottage. He was a valet for the last Lord Stafford at Costessey Hall, 1892 to 1913.

Plate 91

183

The cottage with its gable-end (plate 91) to the roadway is also very old as it is mentioned in the Manorial Court as belonging to John Reade who died in 1666. The 1840 Tithe Award lists John Taylor as owner of this cottage and occupied by Robert Buxton. John Taylor died in 1864, the next owner being the Costessey Estate. At the 1918 sale of the Costessey Estate it was described as a double-fronted cottage with end towards the road and was included with the double-fronted cottage facing the roadway which had been converted into two small cottages. The complete property was bought by Mr Bartlett for £170. Eventually it became owned and occupied by Robert Denmark who left it to his two daughters. They still live in the gable-ended larger cottage and have no plans to sell the roadside double-fronted property.

92
Meadow Land
48 - 58 West End
T.166

George Gunton bought this meadow adjacent to the Red Lion Beer House (94) from John Downes in 1845 by agreement to pay him twenty-two shillings per week for as long as John Downes and his wife lived. As they lived for the next twenty-one years, George Gunton paid a high price for this meadow over that period of time. He developed this meadow land by building two sets of semi-detached cottages (plate 92a). These were rented out to various tenants and, at his death in 1890, were left to his children who continued as landlords to the tenants. The most easterly cottage, number 48, was occupied by the White family from 1889 and Miss Annie White was still living here well into the 1960s but in 1975 Susan Burden acquired it (plate 92b). The adjoining cottage was listed in 1994-1995 as being occupied by David and Sally Ward.

Plate 92a   *Year 1920*

Adjacent to this property and on the meadow land to the west, George Gunton built another pair of semi-detached cottages (now 54-56 West End) and after his death in 1890 his son, Charles Allan Gunton, sold them to Francis and Helen Cole for £200. In 1905 they sold the two cottages for £190 to Francis Kirby, a Norwich cycle dealer. He built a small cottage on to either end of this pair of semi-detached cottages and, on completion in 1920, sold the now four cottages to Angel Jacobs, with the four tenants being John Lyons, Thomas Mann, George Gotts and Edward Gunton. Frederick Cable became the next owner in 1927 for £400 but, after about two months, he sold out to Russell Gould of Model Farm (112) for £600, at which price Sissen and Bugdale of Costessey, builders, acquired them in 1937. At this time only one cottage was occupied by Walter Barber. The remaining three cottages were then sold to Reg Woodbine, Sidney Powles and Walter Jermy and in 1948 the remaining cottage (58 West End) was sold for £300 to Arthur Dack, one of the last tenants of the Falcon Inn (97) who, in 1950, sold to Walter Davison for £450. He died intestate in 1968 when the property was valued at £3,600 but in 1980 his widow sold out to Stephen Harper for £16,000.

This end cottage (58 West End) was finally sold for £55,000 in 1993 to the present day owner, Sharon E. Colk, who kindly loaned me all the legal papers which helped me to correct the 'Gunton Papers' and also to show the rise in property prices over the years from 1890 to 1993.

Plate 92a   *Year 1988*

93
Village Store
60 - 62 West End
T. 166

On the meadow between the semi-detached cottages (92) and the Red Lion Beer House (94) George Gunton had previously built a house in which he lived until his death in 1890. At the rear of this dwelling he built a brick and tiled outhouse with a very elaborate frontal gable-end (plate 93b) which incorporated lettered brickwork spelling out his name and other specimens of decorative brickwork produced at Costessey Brickworks (111).

After his death the property was left to his children who divided the house in which he had lived into two dwellings, the occupiers being Mrs Cole, his daughter, and Alfred Spelman, a postman, who carried letters to and from Norwich. They were followed by Mrs H. Kiddle and Mr Charles

Plate 93a

Plate 93b

Dawson, a Norwich insurance clerk, who then bought the property and lived here until about 1930 when Mr Brand, from Marlingford, took possession. He obtained the services of Mr John Lusher, a builder, who built a timber extension to the front of the house, and Mr Brand opened up the first shop on this site.

Samuel Eke eventually bought the house and shop and was still the owner in the 1960s. Since then, owing perhaps to trade difficulties in connection with newspapers, there have been many owners, some of whom, particularly in the last few years, have stayed for only short periods. Mr Malcolm Warner, after only one year in the business, transferred it in October 1995 to Paul and Carole Bender. They stayed for only a short time when T.& S. News bought the business which then became managed by Mr and Mrs Ogilvie. They moved to Ipswich and the business was sold to Chartwell Trading with Mr Ian Barber being installed as manager. The shop has seen much rebuilding and renovation over the last thirty years.

94
The Red Lion Beer House
64 West End
T. 166

As the Red Lion Beer House was freehold, it is difficult to find much about its past history. The windows and their iron work take the building back to at least the 1700s and even this building is assumed to have replaced an earlier Red Lion which was mentioned in the Manorial Court in 1756 (87).

In the early 1800s Richard Spaul was living here as a beer retailer, to be followed by John Galley, with John Downes as the owner of not only the Red Lion but also the meadow land around it (92). In 1845 he sold the Red Lion to George Gunton, and his son, Edward, then became the beer retailer and he remained here until he died in 1888 when his wife, Charlotte, took over. She was followed by her son, Edward, who carried on the business

Plate 94

as beer retailer until about 1925 when he sold out to Youngs and Crawshay, the Norwich brewers. They eventually gave up the licence at the Red Lion, transferring it to the Crown Public House in New Costessey in 1931. Edward Gunton, the last beer retailer, then acquired the old Red Lion and remained living here until he died in 1951. It was then sold to Mrs Elizabeth Phillips, a secretary for S. & G. Sergents, Engineers Ltd (81).

Mrs Phillips eventually emigrated to Australia and by the 1980s the old Red Lion became unoccupied and in a bad state of repair. It was then acquired by Richard Thwain, a small jobbing builder, who completely renovated the internal construction of the building before selling it in 1994 to Mr Charles Rothery who, in June 1996, sold out to Mr Roger James.

Photograph (94) dated 1951 shows Mrs Phillips and Mr Henry Gunton, retired Parish Clerk and writer of the 'Gunton Papers', looking at the Old Red Lion.

95

68 West End
T.165

When George Gunton bought the property to the west of the Red Lion Beer House in 1845, he proceeded to demolish all the substandard houses dating back to the late 1660s. However, this particular house was saved from demolition because of its more modern construction. It is seen in the centre of (plate 95a), a street scene in West End, and is a red brick house dating to the late 18th century as the gable-ends are finished off at roof level with the attractive brick pattern known as 'tumbling' (20).

The Tithe Award of 1840 lists John Downes as the owner and the occupier as John Spaul, a tailor, who later moved to the old Post Office (77). John Downes sold out to George Gunton in 1845, and George Savage, a harness maker, was the next tenant. He died in the early 1900s and the business was taken over by his son, Charles, who worked in the shed built in the front garden. This shed can be seen in the photograph (95b) to the left of the Red Lion sign post. Charles continued as a harness maker until trade began to fall away and he left to obtain other work.

The house then became occupied by members of the Spaul family whose forebears were blacksmiths (78). By 1961 Thomas Lister had acquired this cottage and he remained here until his death after which he was succeeded by his wife, Dorothy.

Plate 95a   *Year 1900*

Plate 95b   *Year 1925*

192

96 (L)
70 - 74 West End
T.162 and T.164

The old houses on this site, dating back to 1686, were demolished after George Gunton bought them in1845. He then built these unusual ornamental houses using products of his Costessey Brickworks.

Number 70 (T.162) is the rather small double-fronted cottage known for many years as Farthings, the name being incorporated in the ironwork of the front gate. This cottage, with its windows hooded by rectangular moulds, was built in 1849. The two chimney stacks are rounded using bricks showing in relief a few of the emblems used many times during the building of Costessey Hall, such as the Tudor Rose, the Thistle, Clover Leaf, Bunch of Grapes and the Fleur de Lys. On the west-facing wall of a lean-to section of this cottage are numerous scratched names of children dating from 1870 to 1900. This cottage, seen on the left of (plate 95a),

Plate 96a   *Year 1900*

has had many owners over the last few years, many not staying very long. It then became unoccupied for some time until Richard Thwain acquired it after renovating the nearby Red Lion (94). The cottage was then sold in October 1994 to Mr P. Pennellier, who remained living here for the next four years after which he sold the cottage to Andrew and Barbara Coe.

Numbers 72 and 74 (T.164) are of similar construction but built later in 1866. They are semi-detached, each having three bedrooms which was unusual at this period, with the third bedrooms at the back and front over the central section of the houses.

Charles Harvey lived in number 72 for over fifty years carrying on the trade of boot and shoe making in a shed at the rear of his house. He lost his father very early in life and, with his mother and the rest of his family, was moved into a Poor Law Institution and, when old enough, was taught the trade of cobbling. The house, recently owned by Mr and Mrs Anderson who, in 1994, acquired it from John Pechey, has now been sold to Stephen and Donna Rumbelow. It is thought that this property may have been used as a private school between 1870 and 1900 which would account for the names of many children scratched on the wall of the lean-to section of the adjacent cottage, Farthings, 70 West End.

Number 74, the attached half of this house, is owned by Mr Edward Coman. The photograph (96a) shows the Gunton family outside Charles Harvey's house, whilst photograph (96b) shows Charles Harvey and family at his daughter's wedding.

Plate 96b   *Year 1900*

194

97 (L)
The Falcon Inn, 86 West End
T.340

The Falcon Inn is an extremely old building, but the earliest mention of it in official records is in 1725, when Angelica Vincent succeeded to her father's copyhold. Up to 1836 it was listed as The Stafford Arms with the occupier being James Hudson, but by 1845 the name had been changed to The Falcon Inn. James Hudson, who was the occupier during the change of name, stayed on at the Falcon Inn until 1867, when John Laws became the occupier followed by John Lyons in 1883.

John Lyons was a butler with Lord Stafford in his early days, but eventually took over the Falcon Inn and employed Edward Doggett as 'Mine Host' (plate 97a). Mr Lyons was a very fluent and articulate Irishman and he interested himself in local politics. He was a member of the Parish Council serving as Parish Clerk. He also became Overseer which entailed the

Plate 97a   *Year 1910*

Plate 97b   *Year 1900*

collection of the Poor Rate. He became bankrupt in 1912 and quickly made his getaway back to Ireland leaving his wife and daughter in severely reduced circumstances. They then left the Falcon Inn and moved into the Widows' Cottages (106).

After the departure of John Lyons, the Falcon Inn was let to the Peoples' Refreshment House Association, Ltd at a rent of £30 per year and they remained here until the 1918 sale of the Costessey Estate when the Falcon Inn was bought by Morgans Brewery, Norwich for £1,325. James Melton became the first tenant of the new owners and remained until 1934 when a local man, Percy Harvey, took over. He was followed by quite a number of tenants who lasted for only short periods until the 1960s when the Falcon Inn closed, Arthur Dack and M. J. Hubbard being two of the last tenants.

The Falcon Inn was a very busy place during the heyday of Costessey Hall when Royalty and many distinguished guests were entertained at the Hall. The very old Costessey Gyle had its headquarters here from where the annual procession through the village started during the May celebrations (plate 97c) with Snap the Dragon (plate 97d). In the 1880s a local lodge

Plate 97c

of the Manchester Order of Oddfellows was founded here and quickly gained great support until 1911 when the Health Insurance Act came into force. Members then began failing to support the monthly meetings and eventually the lodge, like the Costessey Gyle, ceased its activities.

Sir Alfred J. Munnings, the famous Suffolk painter, stayed here in 1911 for several weeks whilst painting scenes around Costessey. One such painting showed a group of horses and was entitled 'Crossing the Costessey Ford on the Waveney'. It was sold at Christies in 1984 for £45,360. Sir Alfred certainly knew his horses far better than his rivers as the painting was based on the ford crossing the River Tud in Longwater Lane, Costessey.

At the rear of the Falcon Inn was a small public hall in which various village social activities took place and many older residents of Costessey speak of attending dances or local hops here. The stables flanking each side of the front courtyard were also used for sports activities, one favourite game being skittles. These activities came to an end when, at the beginning of the Second World War, accommodation was required for evacuees.

After the war the eastern wing of the stables was used as a motorcycle repair shop but slowly became derelict. The western wing was used by a

Plate 97d

light engineering company running under the name of Ortham Lathes and owned by Mr Trowse. The brewers finally closed down the old Falcon Inn during the 1960s and sold the building and stables to Mr Tunnicliffe. He sold out to Mr and Mrs Alexander in 1981 but at this time both east and west stable wings were in a derelict condition (plate 97b). Planning permission was obtained to renovate these old stables and convert them to residential use. This work was carried out and they are now occupied as residential accommodation, Mr and Mrs Alexander gaining the annual award for improvements to the village from The Costessey Society.

98
Falcon Meadow Cottage and Falcon Row
West End
T.307 and T. 447

About one hundred metres further on past the Falcon Inn was a double-fronted brick and tile cottage named Falcon Meadow Cottage. It stood facing the roadway and built directly into the road edge, the occupier having to step on to the roadway when leaving by the front door. It had two rooms upstairs and two rooms downstairs with outbuildings and a large garden. The 1840 Tithe Award lists Mrs Burcham as the occupier but, at the 1918 sale of the Costessey Estate, the occupier was listed as Mr George Cannell paying a rent of £3 per annum.

About forty metres further on was Falcon Row, a row of three cottages with gable-end on to the road edge, each cottage having one room, pantry and washhouse on the ground floor and two rooms upstairs but no backyard. Before the 1900s they were occupied by Costessey Estate workers, two being John Hostler and Mrs Ann Spauls. At the 1918 sale, the three occupiers were Mrs Burnett, Miss Wymer and Mrs Dack, all paying a rent of £3 per annum, with, as usual, the Estate paying the rates. All this property was demolished after the Second World War.

Plate 98   *Year 1951*

199

99
Thatched Cottages, West End
T.308 and T.448

This pair of semi-detached cottages was next door to the Falcon Row (98) and the 1840 Tithe Award lists two well-known characters of Costessey, Samuel Sissons and William Barnes, as the tenants. They were followed by H. Sissons, an army pensioner, who wore a cocked hat when he acted as Sword Bearer in the Costessey Gyle procession, and Mark Laws, a shoe repairer, who was a very efficient Recorder in the same procession (97).

The thatched cottage had two rooms on the ground floor and two rooms upstairs, whereas the tiled-roof cottage had only one room up and one down. At the 1918 sale both cottages were occupied by the four Trowers sisters who still remained as tenants of R. H. Tebb after he had bought them at the sale for £290. Eventually the properties became very dilapidated, and the site was cleared and used by Potters of Norwich, a firm of tool handle makers, who later sold out for building development.

Plate 99   *Year 1925*

100
The Mettons, 114 - 118 West End
T.574a, T.212 and T.211

This old photograph (100a) taken about 1865 is one of the oldest in this collection and shows five of the six small dwellings that made up the group of buildings called The Mettons. The sixth cottage was at the rear and included the well that supplied the whole group with water. The records of these go well back to the 1600s when Rodger Brown sold them to John Riseborough. The 1840 Tithe Award lists John Kidd as the owner, but in 1865 he sold the two end foreground cottages to George Gunton who, after demolishing them, built himself, by 1870, a more substantial double-fronted house (plate 100b). He died in 1890 when his son, George, became the owner. Mr H. Cann, a motor engineer, was an occupier in about 1933 staying here until about 1950 when he moved to his new house (82). By 1970 the house was owned by Michael White, a solicitor from Norwich, who sold out to Mr Briggs whose widow, Mrs Jacqueline Briggs, is now the owner.

The four remaining cottages owned by John Kidd were left to his daughters when he died in 1864. The tenants at this time were William Barnes (Cole's Castle), J. King, W. Thurston and S. Sissons. His daughters retained the centre cottage (plate 100b) but sold the remaining three to the Costessey Estate. In 1911 the retained centre cottage with the higher single dormer window (plate 100a) was demolished and much old wattle-and-daub construction was exposed with a hurdlework of vertical stakes interwoven with a mixture of clay strengthened with straw and cow hair, and finished off with plaster. After demolition of the old cottage, a more substantial house was built on the site and named Maria Cottage after its owner Maria Laws, who left it to Charles Doggett. By 1961 his son, George, was the owner and he was followed by Mrs Sylvia Doggett who died in 1994. The cottage has now been renovated and is used as a weekend cottage by its London owners.

The remaining three cottages were sold to Mr Simmons at the 1918 Costessey Estate sale when the listed tenants were Mrs Harvey in the rear cottage, Mr Bowles in the small end cottage known as Cole's Castle, as it was built by Charles Cole, and George Carr in the crow-stepped gable cottage, although it was sub-let to Miss Tyrrell. A well-known character of the village, Fred Barnes, aged 91 in 1997and a source of much undocumented information used in this record, tells of his father being born in Cole's Castle, and he is recorded as the occupier in 1864.

The cottages remained in the Simmons family until 1982 when they were sold to Stephen Balls, who demolished the roofs of the two roadside cottages and raised them to the height of the adjacent rebuilt cottages and at the same time converted the pair of cottages into one dwelling. The rear cottage has, with the well, now been demolished.

Plate 100a
Year 1865

Plate 100b
Year 1951

101 (L)
Prudential Cottages, 122 - 124 West End
T. 392 and T. 554

Photograph (100b) shows a steeply-roofed cottage with a crow-stepped gable-end just past the small end cottage of the Mettons (plate 100a). This cottage is one of a pair of semi-detached cottages but obviously built at different periods (plate 101). The first recorded date is 1820 when Thomas Cason acquired it and in 1826 sold it to the Costessey Estate.

The 1840 Tithe Award lists Thomas Kidd, a builder, as occupier and it is quite possible that he built it for the Costessey Estate. Charles Slade, a coachman to Lord Stafford, took over the tenancy and remained here until 1890 when his two nieces, firstly Mrs Neve and then Mrs Burnett, took over. Mr A. Burnett was the tenant at the time of the 1918 sale of Costessey Estate. The cottage was then bought, together with the adjoining cottage, by R. H. Tebb who later sold them to H. C. Greengrass for

Plate 101   *Year 1918*

203

renovation. Herbert Buttress then acquired it but in 1926 sold it to William Palmer. Mr King bought it in 1946 but, after a short time, sold out to Mr Fenn. It is now owned and occupied by Raymond Balls, a retired builder and the building is now much altered.

The adjoining cottage,124 West End, is much older with the earliest recorded date of 1699 when John Carter became the owner. The 1840 Tithe Award lists Thomas Smith as the owner, but his son, William, who succeeded his father, sold it to the Costessey Estate in 1854. At the 1918 sale of the Estate the tenant was listed as Miss Mary Ann Basham.

Some elderly residents speak of this old cottage being used as a collection point for metal tins and aluminium utensils which were thrown through an open window as part of the Second World War effort to provide metal for the production of Spitfire aircraft. A well-known Costessey character, William (Final) Derrick, was living here in the 1960s and his widow, Mrs Derrick, remained here until 1986 when she sold it to Miss Angela Flood, now Mrs Erwin.

102 (L)
Kimberley Farm House & Carpenters' Shop
136 West End
T.343 and T.344

This old farm house (plate 102) is quite long but only one room deep and built right on the road edge. It has retained an oak-raftered ceiling which closely resembles one in the old Tudor Manor House (124). The adjoining carpenters' shop was also of some age before being destroyed by fire in 1890. It had a thatched roof but on rebuilding was roofed with tiles. William Hastings, a builder and farmer, was the occupier, but after his death in 1865 his son, Charles, took over but, being unable to make the business pay, he left Costessey in the early 1870s.

Frederick Gunton took over the building business and, in 1875, was entrusted with the building of Booton Church, Norfolk. Many of the

Plate 102   *Year 1918*

wooden angels for the new church were carved by James Minns in the old carpenters' shop and some were here in 1890 when the shop was destroyed by fire. Frederick Gunton retired in 1902 leaving the business to his two nephews, Charles Gunton and Albert Palmer, who, in 1901, had been entrusted to build the new vicarage (63) in Folgate Lane, Costessey. However, Charles Gunton left the business in 1907 leaving Albert Palmer to carry on alone and only the intervention of his uncle prevented bankruptcy. The building of the two villas (65) was a financial handicap and by 1918 Alfred Palmer had gone out of business.

At the 1918 sale of the Costessey Estate the farmhouse and carpenters' shop found no buyer and was withdrawn at £350. It was later acquired by H. C. Greengrass, Builders, and they sold in 1945 to Norman Bentley of Norwich who died about 1957. He was succeeded by his son, Eric, but much of the land has now been sold for building development.

The rebuilt carpenters' shop has been used for many trades, builders, carpenters, blacksmiths and also wheelwrights who had their large pit in the centre of the rear yard for heating the iron rims prior to fitting them over the rims of the wooden wheels. Also in the outbuildings across the roadway was a vertical saw pit, operated by two men, one above the log of wood and one below in the pit under the log. The circular saw put an end to this method of log sawing. Large drying sheds were also on site for drying and seasoning the sawn planks of wood. At one time the old carpenters' shop was used as a secondhand furniture shop but it is now used entirely by Eric Bentley for his own use.

103
Aerial Photograph

This 1951 aerial photograph shows, at the bottom edge, the old West End Farmhouse (104) and between this building and the next building further along on the right are the smallholdings that at one time were fields belonging to West End Farm. Adjoining these smallholdings and set back from the roadside are the two Laundry Cottages (105).

Close by with its front facing wall built right up to the road edge is the old barn building known as the Widows' Cottages (106). A little further along and set well back from the roadside is a new building, the beginning of postwar development of this area. A short distance further along with its gable-end hard up to the roadside is the old small farm cottage known as The Meads (107), and at the top is Poplar Farm House (108).

Plate 103   *Year 1951*

207

104
West End Farm
T.288

The 1840 Tithe Award lists Costessey Estate as the owner with Robert Barker (8) as the occupier. He was followed in 1864 by Richard White (105). He was an Estate gamekeeper and then head woodman, living in the Keeper's Cottage (69). West End Farmhouse was very small and only one room deep, and Mr White persuaded the Costessey Estate to extend the building at the rear gable-end for additional rooms to house his growing family provided by his three wives. This 1870 extension can be seen on the extreme right of photograph (104b) which now shows the two cottages. Richard White remained at the farm for about twenty years and was followed by John Carr from Common Farm (114). He died in 1888 and his son, George, took over the tenancy and became a very successful dairy farmer.

After the 1918 sale of the Costessey Estate, a firm of tool-handle makers, Tushing of Norwich, acquired it and installed Mr Fox as tenant but some

Plate 104a Rear of West End Farm   *Year 1918*

Plate 104b

time later the farm was split up and sold. Low Brothers of Norwich, corn dealers, bought the farmhouse and divided it into two dwellings for staff employees, Sidney Earl and Charles Crane. Mr Robert Brown bought the farm but on his death his son, Arthur, sold out for building development. Sidney Earl bought the farmhouse cottages in 1961, and, on his death in 1972, his daughter, Mrs Constance Bloom, became owner-occupier. In 1976 the roadside cottage was sold to Elizabeth Piecha who then sold to Mr Keith Houghton. The rear cottage, with cattery, is now owned by Laurence and Christine Bloom.

105
Laundry Cottages
182 - 184 West End
T.300 and T.302

These thatched cottages (plate 105) were listed in the 1840 Tithe Award as Laundry Cottages owned by the Costessey Estate and occupied by Sophia Harris and Elizabeth Dunn. Martha Dunham, who later became the third wife of Richard White (104), lived in one of the cottages for many years and carried on a small laundry business until she died in 1909. Next door lived Mrs George Pratt who also carried on a laundry business, hence the name Laundry Cottages.

The meadow land at the rear of these cottages was also owned by the Costessey Estate and occupied by George Gunton (92) and, after his death in 1890, William Rouse became the new occupier.

Plate 105

At the 1918 Costessey Estate sale Laundry Cottages were combined with the meadow land at the rear of the cottages and sold as one lot. At this time the cottages were occupied by Mrs L. Pratt and Mr B. Dunham at rents of £7 and £6 per annum.

Number 182 has since been re-named as Willow Tree Cottage, and in 1988 was sold by Mr Vincent to Graham and Jeanne Webb. Miss Beatrice Pratt succeeded Mrs L. Pratt and in 1955 sold number 184 to Mr Eric and Sybil Chamberlin. The old Laundry Cottages are still thatched and appear to have been very successfully renovated.

106
The Widows' Cottages, West End
T.324

This old barn (plate 106a) was located midway between West End Farm (104) and Poplar Farm (108). It closely resembled the existing Tithe Barn of Church Farm (47), which was built about the same time, 1685. However, by the end of the 1700s its use as a farm barn is in doubt as, at this period it was converted by the Costessey Estate into accommodation for three Catholic widows. Each widow had only one room with a curtained off part for sleeping, and a small recess for cooking and food storage. Each had her own front door leading directly on to the roadway.

Toilet facilities were in a shed at the rear with the only closet being shared by the three widows, each taking her turn to keep it clean. Water was obtained from a ground-level flap-covered well in the garden of the adjacent property known as The Meads (107). Later on, a water pump was installed against the wall of the adjacent Laundry Cottages (105) and the widows were then allowed to use this pump.

After the death of the last Lord Stafford at Costessey Hall (125) the Widows' Cottages were given in trust to The Catholic Mission in Costessey with the hope that they would maintain them. The rule of only housing Catholic widows was relaxed in order that any poor person could be accommodated here.

When Herbert Cannell was living at the Tudor Manor House (124), the three occupants were invited to his summer garden parties held in the park and some of the last occupiers are seen in photograph (106b). They are Mrs Lyons, left, Miss Kidd, centre and Miss White, a Costessey nurse, who, in her final year, lost her mind and while attempting to walk across Tower Hill woods to her old home, Linall's Lodge (122), lost her life.

Eventually the thatched roof of The Widows' Cottages began to disintegrate and money was not available to repair it and the cottages, now unfit for habitation, were cleared of occupants. The old building began to get very dilapidated and, in 1961, was demolished with the land being cleared for building development.

Plate 106a   *Year 1918*

Plate 106b   *Year 1920*

213

107
The Meads, 190 West End
T. 397

It is more than probable that this house, standing gable-end on to the roadway, was a small farm cottage as a barn type structure adjoined the rear of the building and, showing on the 1840 Tithe Award map, was another barn type building with gable-end on to the roadway. However, this latter building had been demolished before the 1880 Ordnance Survey map had been produced.

The cottage has a curiously-shaped double staircase, an 'x' formation leading up from adjacent ground floor rooms, connecting at the partition wall and then separating to lead into adjacent bedrooms. This would suggest that this cottage was, at one time, two small semi-detached cottages. The 1840 Tithe Award lists the owner as the Costessey Estate with John Laws, an employee of the Estate, as tenant. Later on, in 1868, he is listed as tenant of The Falcon Inn (97).

At the 1918 sale of the Costessey Estate, James Simmons was the listed tenant, and his wife, Mary, is seen standing at the gateway of the cottage (plate 107). The property was bought by R.H. Tebb and it has changed hands several times since the sale. A. J. Notley, a well known local artist, lived here for several years. G. Gibbs bought it from Paul Logie in 1979. Nicholas and Marian White followed in 1987.

214

Plate 107   *Year 1920*

215

108
Poplar Farm, 200 West End
T.38

The 1840 Tithe Award lists Thomas F. Berney is the owner of this farm with Henry Lovett as tenant. He used the farm buildings for his business as a carpenter and builder whilst still living in The Croft (61). His son-in-law, Charles Watcham, followed until his death in 1877. William Cannell, a farmer and butcher, then hired the farm putting his farm foreman, Robert Bush, into the farmhouse until he was replaced by William Long about 1900. He was followed by Charles Slade, a retired coachman from Costessey Hall, but he left soon afterwards when William Rouse moved in. At this time the farm was still owned by the Berney family until sold to William Rouse in 1920. Mr Rouse and his son continued farming until 1930 when William Rouse retired, building himself a bungalow adjacent to Poplar Farm on the south side.

The farmhouse was then divided into two separate dwellings, Mr Drake, a dealer, buying the section on the left and Mr Rix buying that on the right.

Plate 108a

Plate 108b   *Year 1870*

This remained in the Rix family until his death in 1960 when his stepdaughter, Miss Doris George, succeeded and, in 1961, sold to Percy and Caroline Ash. Mr Ash died in 1996 and was succeeded by his widow, Mrs C. Ash. The adjoining cottage is owned by Kevin and Yvonne Spillings. Poplar Farm gets the name from a belt of poplar trees that bordered the roadside at the junction of Taverham Lane (plate 108b). This is a painting by J.S. Corbett, a son-in-law of the Rev. James W. Evans (68).

To the north of Poplar Farm was Costessey Common, but, after the Enclosure Act of 1860, it was awarded to Lord Stafford of Costessey Hall and included with West End Farm (104). Lord Stafford was not in favour of the Enclosure Act and opposed it which resulted in the following letter being published in 'The Norfolk Chronicle',

Honoured Sir,
The poor inhabitants of Costessey humbly beg that you will accept their grateful thanks for your kind and paternal care towards the parish in general, in opposing the intended inclosure of their Common, thereby setting a bright example to the nation in refusing to increase your estate by diminishing the comforts and happiness

of the Poor around you; for this shall your name be handed down to future generations, and while we bless our illustrious Benefactor, our children shall be taught to hail the name of Jerningham as the Shield of the Weak, and Protector of the Poor.

29th Sept 1810
Signed: Matthew Barker   Thomas Cooper   William Hastings

However, Sir George was eventually overruled and the final order of the 11th August 1860 was confirmed on the 7th September 1860.

During the Second World War much sand and gravel was excavated from this additional farm land for the building of airfields and, being very close to the River Wensum, these excavations gradually filled with water. This resulted in lakes being formed, in some parts over 30 feet deep (plate 108c). These lakes are now used by the Anglian Water Authority as a water reservoir. About 1986 a large underground pipe was laid from these lakes into the Norwich water system mainly to bypass any possible leakage or contamination into the river from a downstream chemical factory.

Plate 108c   *Year 1961*

109
Lyth House, Ringland Lane
T. 352 and T. 353

The 1840 Tithe Award lists Lyth House as a smallholding comprising a farmhouse, buildings, orchard, arable land and woodland, all owned by the Costessey Estate and occupied by Mrs Diana Hastings, a daughter of the Costessey farmer and land owner, Eldon Money (57). Diana had married Edward Hastings in 1794 so it is probable that they had farmed here since then.

By 1918 the house had been converted into a pair of semi-detached cottages with a lobby style entrance and was occupied by J. Coward and G. Turner, with the land being let to George Carr, a local farmer. At the 1918 Estate Sale the property was bought by R. H. Tebb for £290. It was eventually sold to Walter Ives who spent a number of years converting the semi-detached cottages back into one dwelling and laying out the garden to a single design before selling it to Mr R. Chamberlain. Walter Ives then bought the adjoining woodland property with the Beehive Lodge (110).

Plate 109

Royston Rowley, a professional photographer, then became the next owner of Lyth House staying here until Walter Ives built a bungalow for him on land between Lyth House and the Beehive Lodge. Lyth House was then sold to Mr Reeve who stayed here for only a short period before selling out to Mr and Mrs Keith King in 1970. About this time an inspector of buildings of architectural interest described Lyth House as a very good example of a lobby-style farmhouse and only the replacement of the old original windows by modern styles prevented the property being listed as a Grade II building. In February 1996 Keith King sold out to Mr and Mrs Duncan Smith.

110 (L)
The Beehive Lodge
Ringland Lane
T. 446

Between 1790 and 1800 Sir William Jerningham built this attractive thatch-roofed round house, now known as the Beehive Lodge, in Blackhill Wood at the extreme north-western end of the Costessey Estate. It was occupied by Estate workers mainly gamekeepers and woodmen. The 1840 Tithe Award lists it as being owned by the Costessey Estate with Charles and Ann Spauls as tenants. In the 1890s a quaint old character named Barber lived here. When younger he would stand in the middle of nine pins (round pieces of wood) and allow a heavy flat piece of wood, called a cheese, to be thrown at the pins in return for a pint of beer. Thomas White lived here for a few years with his aunt, Elizabeth White, and returning home from the village one night in 1905, and most probably from the Falcon Inn, he fell into the river which flows past the property and was drowned. He was only 49 years of age.

Plate 110a   *Year 1918*

At the 1918 sale of Costessey Estate the lodge was unoccupied (plate 110a) and was included with the whole of Blackhill Wood, but finding no buyer it was withdrawn only to be sold separately about a year later to R. H. Tebb. It then changed hands many times, with Capt. George (Cox) Starling taking up residence in the 1930s.

Walter Ives (109) bought it in the early 1950s and started a large scale development programme, enlarging the lodge and building additional accommodation (plate 110b). After the death of Mr Ives in 1961, his widow remained living at Beehive Lodge until the early 1990s. The property was put up for sale but, owing to difficulties over boundaries through Blackhill Wood, the exchanging of contracts with a potential purchaser was very protracted. In 1993 a group of New Age travellers on the nearby Ringland Hills did little to enhance the attractiveness of the Beehive Lodge. The vandalism could only be rectified after the contracts had been signed and the New Age travellers officially removed.

In April 1995 Sean and Kathryn Parry moved in to commence their planned renovation of the Beehive Lodge. In November 1995 they gained recognition in the Norfolk Society's annual awards for projects that are aimed at preserving Norfolk's heritage, with a special commendation for the renewal of the thatched roof to the original lodge. After the completion of the planned renovation the Beehive Lodge was sold to Mr William Annette from Vancouver, Canada.

Plate 110b

111
Brickyard House, West End
T. 335

Brickyard House, the home of past owners of the Costessey Brickworks, has seen many changes over the years. In the late 1700s it was a very small bungalow of two rooms and a lean-to kitchen with outside toilet and washroom. In 1830 the Costessey Estate, who owned the brickyard site, asked George Gunton (1st) to take over the running of the brickworks, and, with his young wife, he moved into this very small bungalow, and here he started to raise a very large family. This made it necessary to build an extension to the bungalow, but even this became insufficient for his family, some of whom were then required to sleep in the attic space which had neither windows nor ventilation.

In 1861 George Gunton left this small bungalow and moved into a house that he had built next door to the Red Lion Beer House (93). He retired

Plate 111   *Year 1951*

from the brickworks in 1868 leaving his son, George (2nd), as manager. He was followed by his son, George (3rd), as manager who, in about 1890, stripped off the roof of the bungalow, extended the ground floor accommodation and built four upper-storey rooms (plate 111). Here George Gunton (3rd) lived and, in partnership with his brother William who would later buy Wensum Cottage (33), managed the brickworks up to 1909 when George left leaving his brother, William, as sole owner.

Brickyard House was then let to William Rouse, a farmer (108), as tenant of the Costessey Estate, and Henry Gunton, son of William , carried on as the manager of the brickworks until it closed in 1916. At the 1918 sale of the Estate, Brickyard House and yard was sold to George Carr, a local farmer, for £670. The brickyard was then cleared and turned over to farming. After the death of George Carr in 1934, his son, Walstan, took over the farm until his death in 1985. His widow succeeded and remained living in Brickyard House until 1996 when she sold out to a builder, Richard Sporle, who intends to renovate the building for sale.

The track leading from West End to the junction with the brickyard now continues on to Crete Lodge (plate 112c) and Model Farm (plate 112b).

112 (L)
Brick Farm and Model Farm
Brickfield Loke West End
T.375, T.366 and T.367

The continuation of Brickfield Loke led to Brick Farm owned by the Costessey Estate and farmed by John Harman who, in the 1840 Tithe Award, is listed as living in the old Tudor Manor House, then known as Home Farm (124). He, with his brother, Henry, owned much land in Costessey (115-116). After 1840 the Estate built further farm buildings and two semi-detached cottages for stockmen(plate 112a) and this allowed John Harman to keep cattle on Brick Farm.

After the 1918 sale of Costessey Estate, Mr R. Gould, a Norwich accountant, bought the farm and established a Model Dairy here selling better class milk at more than the standard price. A new house was built near the dairy for an employee (plate 112b left), and a larger house (plate 112c) for the farm manager, Mr Smith.

Plate 112a   *Year 1918*

113 (L)
Costessey Lodge, Dereham Road
T.401

At the south-western corner of Costessey Park and adjacent to the parish boundary with Easton is Costessey Lodge. It was designed by the architect of Costessey Hall, John Chessell Buckler, and was built in the early 1830s. It was described as being very well built, containing two rooms, kitchen and pantry on the ground floor, with three bedrooms and a tower room above. It was designed for a lodge gatekeeper and a gamekeeper who could have been one and the same person or husband and wife but, in 1864, Robert Charles Rising, a farmer, was listed as being the tenant. It continued as such until the death of the last Lord Stafford at Costessey Hall in June 1913.

At the 1918 sale of the Costessey Estate it was put up for sale together with the vast expanse of the park woodland and the large mansion, Costessey Hall. No buyer could be found so the lodge was disjoined from

Plate 113   *Year 1951*

the park and Hall and sold off with an acre of ground to Mr J. Morse, a nurseryman of Eaton, near Norwich, who then had the acre of land well laid out as a garden.

The next owner-occupier was Mr A. E. Priest, a Norwich motor car and motorcycle engineer, who had, in 1948, sold his previous residence, Eastwood Lodge (68) to Mr E. E. Hines, also a Norwich engineer. Mr Priest died in the late 1950s and his widow moved from Costessey Lodge and back to a new bungalow built on the site of Denny's Cottage (69) adjacent to Eastwood Lodge (68).

Mr L. H. Gunton of Gunton's Driving School, Norwich, then acquired the lodge. He made many improvements to the building including extra accommodation. After the death of his wife, he remained living at the lodge until his death in November 1994. The lodge was then advertised for sale as a 'Fairytale Castle in Costessey', a very apt description because of its elaborate design. It was sold to Mark and Sarah Alden who are carrying out an extensive internal rebuilding scheme.

114
Common Farm, Townhouse Road
T.158 and T.159

At the eastern corner of Folgate Lane and its junction with Townhouse Road was Common Farm the records of which go back to the 1600s. It came into the Carr family when Isaac Cannell bought it in 1826 for £375 and then passed it over to his daughter, Mary Carr. The 1840 Tithe Award lists John Carr as the owner and occupier and he,with his son John, farmed here for many years until they sold out to the Costessey Estate in 1865. They then left Common Farm to take over West End Farm (104) and a cow-keeper, Mr Whall, moved in as tenant at Common Farm and stayed here for a number of years.

During the First World War, the farmhouse was occupied by Mrs Barber whose grand -daughter lost her life in the sinking of the 'Lusitania' on her

Plate 114

way back home to Costessey. At the 1918 sale of the Costessey Estate the farm was again in the occupation of the Carr family, with George Carr as tenant paying a rent of £12 per annum. The farm and farmhouse, built in 1825, was bought by J. Blake for £290. His brother, Walter, lived here for several years followed by his sister who left after the Second World War, the farm lands being sold off for building sites.

In 1961 the farmhouse, now known as Hillcrest, was occupied by Harvey Pearson who sold it in 1977 to Professor Brian Moss, a biologist at the University of East Anglia. On his moving to Liverpool in 1989, the property was bought by John Wrath on behalf of Hendon Decorators Ltd and is now owned by Godstone Properties as a letting agent. In 1990 it was rented out to Shell Oil Company with a marine biologist, Dr Frans Holman, in residence. In January 1996 Mrs Judy Mears with her husband and daughter took up residence and she has reported that a certain atmosphere in the ground floor living room, with unaccountable shadowy movements across the room towards the cellar door, conveys a sensation of the room being haunted. Likewise, the next door property, Glenhurst, which was built on the foundations of the old farm barns, has recently been subjected to ghostly apparitions. These spectral visitations, according to the occupier, John Wrath, became apparent after he had located and disturbed an ancient well on the site.

115
Beech House, Townhouse Road
T.199

The 1840 Tithe Award lists John Harman as the owner of Beech House with Peter Howard as the occupier. John Harman farmed large areas of land mainly in what is now New Costessey owning most of the land and renting some from the Costessey Estate (112) and (124).

William Kuppers bought Beech House with much other property about 1910 and lived here until his death in 1929, his eldest son, William, taking over and carrying on a business of pig farming at the nearby Ferrybridge Farm, now known as Bridge Farm (116). The business failed with William running into financial difficulties. He then committed suicide by swallowing a poisonous liquid, and was found dead in his garden.

After the suicide of William Kuppers in the early 1930s, Beech House was sold to Mr H. Wells, a Norwich corn merchant, to be followed by Mrs Watcham, G. Addison and Geoffrey Towler. In 1968 it was sold to Dominic Conway of Dipple and Conway Norwich Ltd, Ophthalmic Opticians. After he retired in 1987, Beech House was taken over by his son, Damian, who has now renovated the building to modern standards.

Plate 114

116
Bridge Farm
161 Norwich Road, New Costessey
T.189

Although locally known as Green's Farm and situated just over the River Tud in New Costessey, Bridge Farm is included in this record because of its group value with Beech House (115). From records we find that, in 1810, Robert Silvey obtained possession of about 8 acres of land called The Little Fields with the adjoining meadows. In 1825 he sold this property to Joseph Harman for £600 but the sale included all farm buildings, so it can be assumed that Robert Silvey built what was then known as Ferrybridge Farm. On the death of Joseph Harman in 1829, John Harman succeeded but by 1840 the Tithe Award lists Henry Harman as the owner and occupier. At this time, John Harman was the tenant occupier of the Tudor Manor House, then known as Home Farm (124) in Costessey Park.

William Kuppers, a farm bailiff, took over Bridge Farm in about 1910 and eventually became owner, when he started off the business of pig farming,

Plate 116

pig killing and sausage-skin making. After the untimely death of his son, William (115), his next son, Ernest, took over the running of the business. The farm was then let to Sidney Green whose son, Robert, bought the farm in 1961. After his death in 1984, his eldest son, also named Robert, took over the farm. The old farmhouse was demolished and, in 1987, a modern farmhouse built. A new building designed as a farm shop was built near the dairy sheds and run by Robert Green with the help of Mrs Green (senior) but it met with only limited success. The shop was then let to various tenants but again the business did not reach the required returns and the shop was closed.

In 1990 Robert Green (junior) died and he was succeeded by his brother, Martin, who took over the running of the farm. In 1995 the unoccupied farm shop was let out as a car boot shop, but it was realised that an official change of use had to be applied for. This action was considered not worth the trouble and, again, the shop was closed.

In 1988 two fishing lakes were developed, one for trout and the other for coarse fishing. Much more recently the dairy herd was disposed of and the meadow land broken up. Some was sold for housing development and some has been divided into paddocks for letting to pony owners. In 1996 a further housing development scheme was applied for.

117 (L)
The Roundhouse, 457 Dereham Road
T.309 and T.310

Opposite the Roundwell Obelisk and on the south side of the Norwich to Dereham road stands an octagonal building known as the Roundhouse. By its unusual design it appears to have been built by Sir William Jerningham in the 1790s to accommodate two farm workers from Lodge Farm. The 1840 Tithe Award lists the Costessey Estate as the owner with Charles Beloe and John Galley as the tenants. Each of the two cottages had only three rooms with outside washhouse and earth closet. Water was obtained from the historic well known as the Round Well (118).

At the 1918 sale of the Costessey Estate no occupants were recorded but the Roundhouse was bought by Mr L. Bowles of Norwich together with about twenty-six acres of land for which he paid £960. He then moved into one of the cottages and sold off the land for building development.

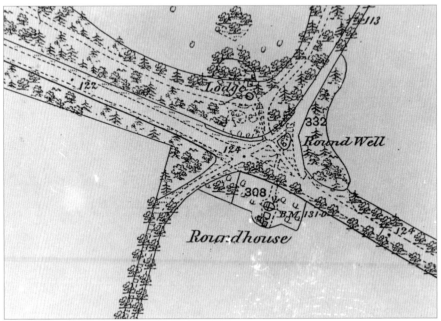

Plate 117a   *Year 1880*

Plate 117b   *Year 1918*

In the 1960s Mr and Mrs George Paul were the occupiers for a number of years until an American couple took over for a short period. They were followed by Mr and Mrs Geoffrey Little who, in 1990, sold out to Graham and Sheila Jones. The Roundhouse has, for many years, been occupied as a single dwelling, perhaps reconstructed by Mr L. Bowles.

The current register of listed buildings produced by the South Norfolk District Council refers to this building as a former Toll House and states that it is marked as a Toll House on the 1840 Tithe Map. There is no mention of it being a Toll House under Tithe Award numbers 309 and 310 which were allocated to the two small farm cottages that made up this one dwelling place. It is also not shown as a Toll House on either the 1839 Ordnance Survey Tithe Map or the 1840 sketch map of the Tithe Apportionment, both of which are in the writer's possession.

The Roundhouse has since been much enlarged and renovated as has the similar type of building known as the Beehive Lodge (110) which was also built by Sir William Jerningham at this same period in the 1790s.

118 (L)
The Round Well
T.529
and Round Well Lodge
Longwater Lane
T.400

Standing at the south end of Longwater Lane near its junction with the Norwich to Dereham Road is an obelisk known as the Round Well. In the late 1790s, Sir William Jerningham, of Costessey Hall, built the small lodge guarding the entrance to the park at this point and also the Roundhouse (117) opposite. It is, therefore, reasonable to assume that he also had the well sunk on the location of a known spring to provide water for these isolated properties.

About 1820, during the Napoleonic Wars, French prisoners of war were put to work building a brick and stone plinth around the base of this well.

Plate 118   *Year 1918*

On top of this they built a brick and stone column some twelve feet high and topped it with a stone urn. Access to the water was via a large opening in the side of the plinth.

At the 1918 sale of Costessey Estate, the Round Well Lodge was sold to E. Morse, but it was eventually owned by Herbert Cannell who sold it with sufficient land to Steward and Patteson, Brewers of Norwich, and by the early 1930s the old lodge had been demolished and the Round Well Public House opened. Mr L. Bowles, who had bought the Roundhouse opposite and then sold off parts of the land as building plots, still had rights of access to the Round Well. These rights also extended to any building on these plots, so that, when Steward and Patteson endeavoured to enclose the well, the Costessey Parish Council prevented this action.

The water, however, was often fouled by rubbish thrown into the well by persons unknown, which led to some friction. This fortunately ceased when water mains were extended to this area in 1935. It was a tremendous relief to those who habitually lost their pails down the well because of the awkward access to the water.

No photograph can be found of the Round Well Lodge, but the 1840 Tithe Award lists Joseph Laws as the occupier. John Gunton lived here in the 1880s followed by Frederick Kidd. The 1918 sale catalogue describes it as having only two rooms, both on the ground floor, with outside wash-house, earth closet and garden, which was similar to the other round houses built by Sir William Jerningham in the 1790s (110), (117) and (123).

The Round Well obelisk has needed much maintenance over the years. The last major repair was in 1981 when the complete column with urn was demolished and rebuilt in brickwork by the Parish Council. Motorists driving along the Norwich to Dereham road perhaps pass this obelisk without giving it a second thought.

119
Longwater Lane Bridges

The building of the first footway bridge over the River Tud where it crossed Longwater Lane has been attributed to Sir William Jerningham in about 1793. There is an abundance of photographs in the writer's collection of these footway bridges, but only a few of these can be used to show the various types of construction. They are :-

A. The earliest photograph known of the Carriers' or Stick Bridge photographed in 1858 by Dr Michael Beverley, a dental surgeon from Norwich. View looking upstream towards Costessey Hall. As this bridge appears to be in good condition, it may be assumed that it was built about this time.

B. Carriers' or Stick Bridge and Ford photographed about 1880. View looking towards Costessey village. As the stick construction design has changed from the 1858 design, it may be assumed that this photograph was taken much later.

Plate 119a   *Year 1858*

C. As stick bridges required regular maintenance, a stronger rustic constuction was employed. Here is a humped-back rustic bridge which proved difficult to cross by mothers pushing prams.

D. To overcome this difficulty the bridge was modified to create a level footway. This photograph was taken about 1905 with the view looking towards Costessey village. Note the old National Telegraph Company's pole in the background trees. This pole served only two subscribers, most probably at Costessey Hall.

E. The Concrete and Iron Bridge photographed in 1910 by Francis Welch (77). This bridge was built about 1907 to replace all the old wooden bridges that, in the past, had caused so much maintenance work to be carried out. However, it did not last very long, being destroyed in the 1912 floods as was the brick bridge over the River Tud against Bridge Farm (116). View looking towards the Round Well.

F. The first Carriage-way Bridge built in 1913 to replace the concrete and iron bridge. Photographed by Francis Welch with the view looking towards the Round Well. Date not recorded, but about 1925 or a little later.

Plate 119b   *Year c. 1880*

Plate 119c   *Year 1900*

Plate 119d   *Year 1905*

Plate 119e   *Year 1910*

Plate 119f   *Year c. 1925*

120
River Views, Longwater Lane

This painting (plate 120a) from a vantage point on one of the stick bridges shows an early waterfall erected to create an artificial lake in front of the old Tudor Hall seen on the left against a bank of distant trees. The date is not recorded but it is well before the start of the large extension to the old hall in1827 (125).

During Sir George Jerningham's time, 1809 - 1851, a more substantial waterfall was built (plate 120b) creating a much wider artificial lake. The gates in the foreground were to keep the debris from fouling the ford at this point and would be opened at convenient times to allow the accumulation of debris to float downstream.

The artificial lake was kept clear of vegetation especially by the last Lord Stafford but, after his death in 1913, maintenance of the lake ceased and,

Plate 120a   *Year c. 1825*

Plate 120b   *Year 1910*

Plate 120c   *Year 1951*

243

Plate 120d   *Year c. 1900*

during the Second World War when all types of metal were required, the iron railings of the waterfall were taken (plate 120c). By 1951, when this photograph was taken, the sluice gate in the waterfall had gone together with the large artificial lake and the greater part of Costessey Hall, leaving just the Thornbury Tower and the Clock Tower standing. Only the old clock tower now remains, the old waterfall weir having been demolished during the building of the new road bridge that bypasses the old carriage-way bridge seen on photograph (119f).

Leaving the old Longwater Lane bridges about the turn of the 20th century (plate 120d) and proceeding towards West End, we see the Costessey Park boundary fence on top of a high grass bank. This bank still exists at the entrance to the Longwater Lane Recreation Ground.

121
Head Gardener's House
Costessey Hall
T.491 and T.492

The 1840 Tithe Award lists John Wigton as the tenant in the old head gardener's house seen behind the larger cottage in the foreground (plate 121). After his death in 1878 a gardener named Burberry took over for a short time until Andrew Roach became the head gardener. He was followed by Walstan White who died in 1905.

Michael Quinn then arrived from Ireland and occupied the old cottage. A very good gardener, he exhibited and won prizes at many local shows. During his time, the Costessey Estate built a larger cottage for the head gardener in front of the old cottage. This has a date stone near the top of the front gable, dated 1914, which shows that this cottage was not completed until after the death of the last Lord Stafford at Costessey Hall in June 1913.

Plate 121   *Year 1951*

At the Costessey Estate sale in 1918 the gardener's house was sold to John B. Jones of Yorkshire and Michael Quinn moved to Swynnerton Park as head gardener to the new Lord Stafford. John Jones then started up as a market gardener. He made an access driveway through Snakes Hills to the Brick Farm driveway (111). However, his efforts at market gardening met with little success and he sold out to J. Jarvis who made a new access driveway over Tower Hill to West End.

The Jarvis family were here for a number of years and we must assume that they built the three bay windows shown in this 1951 photograph (121) and it is more than likely that they later built the fourth and matching bay window over the bedroom window on the right, which exists today. They eventually sold out to Mr Littleboy who then let the property to Mr Spooner, a gardener and nurseryman. The property eventually passed to Littleboy's son-in-law, John Jeffreys, who, about 1970, sold out to Mr and Mrs Boast. It is still in the Boast family being owned jointly by the sons, who planned to sell the property during 1997.

122
Linall's Lodge, Costessey Park
T.398

The original driveway to the old Tudor Manor House (124) and the New Hall (125) turned off West End about opposite the Mettons (100). Part of this driveway is shown on an Estate plan drawn up for Sir George Jerningham, 5th Baronet, in about 1750. The lodge, guarding this driveway, was set well back into a belt of trees bordering West End. Sir George died in 1774 and was succeeded by Sir William Jerningham who decided to build two extra driveways, one to the Norwich to Dereham road where the Roundhouse (117) and the Roundwell Lodge (118) were built, and the other driveway to Costessey village with entrance gates opposite the Falcon Inn (plate 97a).

After the opening of the Falcon driveway (plate 123a) in the 1790s the old driveway to Linall's Lodge became disused, and is not shown on the 1840 Tithe Award map nor on the 1880 Ordnance Survey map. However, what appears to be a part of the old lodge is seen to the left of and adjoining the later more substantial lodge in photograph (plate 122). This lodge was built in the mid 1800s and was occupied by James Linall, a woodcarver at Costessey Hall, and for many years this lodge was known as Linall's Lodge with the belt of trees, in which this lodge stood, known as Linall's Belt.

Other occupiers of this lodge were Nurse White who lost her life trying to find her way back to her old home via Tower Hill (106), John Thurston and Charles Slade (108) who was followed by his niece, Lillian Sharpe. She was the last occupier before the lodge was demolished for the development of Parklands.

Plate 122   *Year 1951*

247

123
The Falcon Lodge
Costessey Park
T.325

The Falcon Lodge, like the Roundwell Lodge (118), was built by Sir William Jerningham in about 1793. It was octagonal in shape, built of brick and slate, and only one storey high. The accommodation originally comprised of only two rooms with wash-house and earth closet outside. In 1793 Parson Woodforde of Weston Longville was invited by Sir William Jerningham to inspect the new lodges, and he described them as being 'very handsome'.

The 1840 Tithe Award lists John Daynes as the occupier of The Falcon Lodge and from his time the belt of trees running from the lodge to Longwater Lane was known as Daynes Plantation. Other occupiers after John Daynes were Walstan White (121) followed by Leonard Clarke, both of whom were occupiers for long periods.

Plate 123a   *Year 1905*

Plate 123b   *Year 1981*

During the First World War when Costessey Hall and parkland were commandeered by the War Office, it is reasonable to assume that the Falcon Lodge was used as a guard-house, being so conveniently located on the left of the entrance to the training grounds of Costessey Park (plate 123a).

At the 1918 Estate sale the lodge was put up for auction as a separate unit but, finding no buyer, it was included in the 174 acres of Home Farm and Agent's House and was bought by J. W. Gilbert. It then remained part of the Home Farm Estate until 1981 when, after the death of Captain Dawson in 1979, Mrs Dawson sold part of the farm to Colin House (124). Mrs Dawson retained the old Falcon Lodge as her own property and accommodation for a longtime employee and sitting tenant, Mr F. C. Denny.

By the early 1980s, the development of Parklands had made it necessary to demolish the old lodge and entrance gates to the park. With this in mind Captain Dawson, in the late 1970s, had arranged for a new lodge to be built further into the park and new entrance gates to be provided and, in 1981, Mr and Mrs Denny and family moved from the old lodge into this new building. Photograph (123b) shows the Denny family at the front of the old lodge prior to moving into the nearby larger building.

124 (L)
Tudor Manor House
Costessey Park
T.362

This old Tudor Manor House now known as Costessey Park House is probably the oldest building in Costessey dating back to the 1450 period. According to Colonel Glendenning, an authority on Tudor buildings, it was a Tudor Great Hall with its main central area open from the ground floor up to the timbered roof structure for which one bracket remains in an upstairs passage way.

Some time in the early Stuart period, this house was modified and the Great Hall converted into a dining room with bedrooms and passages above. A chimney was inserted, cutting through the beams of the original roof. The roof pitch was altered and perhaps the gables were built out at the same time. Further alterations were made in the 18th century when

Plate 124a   *Year 1951*

the medieval kitchens etc. were replaced by new kitchens and a brewhouse. It was completely refurbished in the 19th century. The front is of the late Gothic style as are the two axial chimney stacks with 'Cosseyware' chimney pots. No original windows remain but the two rear entrance doors appear to be of the 17th century.

The 1840 Tithe Award lists John Harman (112) and (115) as occupier, but in 1860, by which time Sir Henry Valentine had succeeded his father, Sir George, at Costessey Hall, the old Manor House was occupied by Henry Snelling, listed as farm bailiff for Home Farm . At this time the farm employed seventeen men, six boys and ten women. In 1884 Sir Henry Valentine died and the old Tudor Manor House was taken over by Joseph Coverdale and Son, acting as agents to the Costessey Hall Estate. The old Tudor Manor House then became known as "The Agent's House".

The farm and estate continued to be under the control of the Coverdales and on the Bank Holiday in August 1888 they organised the Costessey Races in the park when eight races were held . A race card found at the old Falcon Inn (97) lists the races as:-

Race for Ponies, not exceeding 12 hands high
Race for Donkeys, distance 1/4 mile.
A foot race for men, distance 1/4 mile
Race for Cobs not exceeding 14 hands high distance one and a half miles
A hurdle race for men, distance 1/2 mile
Race for Hunters, a steeplechase course, distance 2 miles
Race for Donkeys, distance 3/4 mile
Race for Cobs not exceeding 14 hands high, distance one and a half miles.

Conditions
All Jockeys to ride in colours declared at the time of entry.
Any Jockey riding in false colours to be fined 5/-.
All competitors in the foot races to be decently attired.
Those not complying will not be allowed to run.

The Race meeting concluded with the "Pig over the River" for which there were four competitors - W. Paul, C. Paul, T. Ribbons and G. Barley and all had to crawl along a pole suspended over the River Tud to release the captive pig in the basket at the end of the pole.

Plate 124c   *Year 1951*

252

Sir FitzOsbert Edward took over at Costessey Hall in 1892 and the Coverdales moved from the Agent's House with Mr and Mrs Riley, relations of the Jerninghams,moving in. They stayed here until the death of Sir FitzOsbert Edward, the last Lord Stafford at Costessey Hall, in 1913. During the First World War the Agent's House was taken over by the War Office together with the park and Costessey Hall (125) and were retained until the end of the war.

At the sale of Costessey Estate in November 1918, the old Agent's House and Home Farm were sold to J. Wilson Gilbert for £3,960. The next owner was William Cannell, a Costessey butcher and farmer, and he was followed by his son, Herbert. After his death, the farm and house were sold to Mr Riches who, after carrying out further renovations to the old Tudor Manor House (Agent's House), sold out to Capt. Dawson, a Norwich businessman and farmer. He greatly improved the farm and parkland and started off a large pig-rearing unit. He also brought back the old race meetings by arranging a gymkhana and fete annually in August.

After the sudden death of Capt. Dawson in 1979, his widow remained living at the old Tudor Manor House, now re-named Costessey Park House, until 1981 when the property, apart from the old Falcon Lodge (123), was sold to Colin House who continued working the pig unit until it was superseded, in 1984, by the Costessey Park Golf Club. In 1997 the Tudor Manor House together with the Costessey Park Golf Club was sold to an LJ Group Company and the old Manor House became part of Costessey Manor Park, the home to Costessey Park Golf Club Ltd with Mr Colin House retained as Course Manager.

Standing high on Tower Hill behind Costessey Park House was the tall circular brick tower (plate 124b). Built by Sir William Jerningham in 1791, it had two floors with an observation floor at the top from which extensive views as far as Norwich could be obtained. The tower (plate 124c) remained on Tower Hill until its condition became very dangerous and was finally demolished in January 1972. To the north of Costessey Park House is a range of Class II listed farm buildings built by Sir William Jerningham in 1784 but, after the death of Capt. Dawson in 1979, the listed buildings began to deteriorate and, in September 1996, a suspected arson attack was made on the hay-stocked stables. These were virtually destroyed but all other buildings were saved and are now being renovated to comply with listed building requirements.

125 (L)
Costessey Hall, Costessey Park
T.503

Although a recent history of Costessey Hall was published in 1991, it may be of interest to recall a few of the salient features and expand on those that, of necessity, had to be condensed. The old Tudor Manor House (124), which stood on the north side of the River Tud, was granted to Sir Henry Jernegan by Queen Mary in 1555. After her death in 1558, Sir Henry moved to Costessey to build his 'New Hall' on the south side of the River Tud. It was completed in 1564 with the old Manor House being relegated to being the Dower House. In 1825, Sir George Jerningham became the 8th Baron Stafford and, in 1827, started the building of the large extension to the New Hall seen in the photograph (plate 125a) taken from the top of the round Costessey Tower on Tower Hill (plate 124b). Photograph (125b) shows the 1564 New Hall in the foreground with the new extension of 1827 onwards in the background. A western view of this large extension is seen in (plate 125c).

Plate 125a   *Year 1918*

254

Plate 125b   *Year 1910*

Sir George's son, Sir Henry Valentine 9th Baron Stafford, although twice married, produced no heir to carry on a direct line of succession. The heir apparent was his nephew, The Right Hon. Augustus Frederick Fitzherbert Jerningham, a person of unsound mind. Realizing the implication of a suspected lunatic becoming the 10th Baron Stafford with the right to take his seat in the House of Lords, Sir Henry Valentine, on the 20th January 1862, made out a petition requesting that the Masters of Lunacy might be directed to enquire and certify the lunacy of the suspected lunatic.

Francis Barlow and Samuel Warren, the Masters of Lunacy, were then ordered, in pursuance of the General Commission under the Great Seal of Great Britain, to enquire concerning the alleged lunacy of the supposed lunatic, an inmate of Brooke House Asylum, Clapston, Middlesex. On the 19th February 1862, the assumed lunatic was examined and found to be of unsound mind.

On the 30th November 1884, Sir Henry Valentine died and the now official lunatic inherited Costessey Hall, and, if he were to die intestate, the contents of the hall would have to be divided between his brother and many relations, which would leave his brother, The Right Hon. FitzOsbert Edward Jerningham, an empty hall to inherit. The new Lord Stafford

Plate 125c Year 1909

was, therefore, re-examined and he expressed his dislike of living at Costessey Hall as it was not adapted for his residence due to its isolated position with its distance from public entertainments which were his principal pleasures. Without a resident family and frequent visitors he ran the risk of serious injury to himself, the hall and its valuable contents.

It was then decided to close up Costessey Hall but Edward Boardman, a Norwich architect, suggested that this would be very unwise, listing many reasons against closure. On the 4th April 1885 it was decided to purchase the contents and furniture of Costessey Hall with the view that it should remain at the Hall for the use of the new tenant, William Christie, who had made an inventory of the contents to the value of £4,670.

On the 27th April 1885, an official Order in Lunacy was issued in London that the custody of Lord Stafford, a person of unsound mind, be granted to Basil Fitzherbert and Lord Lovat and that they should raise the necessary money to purchase the furniture and contents of Costessey Hall, the money going to the credit of the lunatic Lord Stafford. This they did and the furniture and contents were saved for future use of tenants and put under the control of the committee, named as Basil Fitzherbert and The Right

Hon. Simon Lord Lovat, both relatives of the lunatic Lord Stafford. Under this arrangement with Joseph Coverdale and Son as local agents, the life of Costessey Hall continued. Three years later, in 1888, the Costessey Races (124) were held in the park.

Lord Stafford, 10th Baron Stafford, the person of unsound mind, died in 1892 with his brother, The Right Hon. FitzOsbert Edward Jerningham succeeding and becoming the 11th Baron Stafford at Costessey Hall. He died in June 1913 unmarried, thus leaving no direct heir. The Hall and title of Lord Stafford then passed to his nephew, Lieut. Col. Francis Fitzherbert of Swynnerton Park, Staffordshire, but the contents of the Hall became the property of Mr Stafford Henry Jerningham who, on the death of the last Lord Stafford at Costessey Hall, succeeded to the title of Sir Henry Jerningham 11th Baronet. He then arranged for all the furniture and contents to be sold in December 1913 and the Hall was cleared. With the Military occupation of the Hall from 1914 to 1918 causing much locally recorded damage and the failure of many attempts to sell the empty Hall, it was decided to sell to a firm of demolition contractors, and this ostentatious jewel amongst the old buildings of Costessey listed in this record was brought to an untimely and inglorious end.

Plate 125d   *Year 1987*

All that now remains of this splendid architectural wonder (plate 125a) is the Belfry Tower (plate 125d), which, if local tradition is to be believed, is haunted by a spectral lady dressed in green. Ghosts apart, Costessey park is now home to Costessey Park Golf Club which, in July 1997, was purchased by the Norwich based LJ Group whose aim is to make it one of the best golf courses in Norfolk.